KALEIDOSCOPIA!

KALEIDOSCOPIA!

EVERYTHING YOU NEED TO KNOW ABOUT KALEIDOSCOPES (INCLUDING HOW TO MAKE YOUR OWN!)

CAROLYN BENNETT

WORKMAN PUBLISHING · NEW YORK

Library of Congress Cataloging-in-Publication Data is available.

ISBN 978-0-7611-7293-2

Workman books are available at special discounts when purchased in bulk for premiums and sales promotions as well as for fund-raising or educational use. Special editions or book excerpts can also be created to specification. For details, contact the Special Sales Director at the address below, or send an email to specialmarkets@workman.com.

Cover Design by Raquel Jaramillo
Design by Tae Won Yu

Photography and illustrations: Tae Won Yu
Additional illustrations: Phil Conigilaro
Additional Photography: Courtesy of Cozy Baker, p. 5; Courtesy of Carolyn Bennett, p. viii, p. 1.
© Fotolia: pp. 4, 6, 10, 17, 14, 23, 29, 30, 34, 44, 45, 46, 122, 124. Shutterstock: © Anggaradedy, p. 45 (aluminum bag); © Coprid, p. 45 (plastic roll); © bluesnote, p.123 (glowsticks)

Workman Publishing Co., Inc.
225 Varick Street
New York, NY 10014-4381
workman.com

WORKMAN is a registered trademark of Workman Publishing Co., Inc.

Printed in China
First printing September 2014

10 9 8 7 6 5 4 3 2 1

I dedicate this book to my daughter:
Ana Frances Beatriz Colon Lopez Bennett Kramer.

CONTENTS

Carolyn's Kaleidoscope Designs

Take a look at some of my original creations.

Crystal Vision Teleidoscope

Luna Kaleidoscope

The Barry Kaleidoscope

The Quadra: four kaleidoscopes in one!

Escape Kaleidoscope

Infinity Kaleidoscope

Space Needle Kaleidoscope

Futura Marble Kaleidoscope

INTRODUCTION

A kaleidoscope can be a simple device—as basic as a cardboard tube, two or three mirrors, and some pieces of plastic. But when you put the pieces together just right, the result is a peek into a magic world. All at once, a kaleidoscope reveals a blizzard of colored snowflakes, a tube full of fireworks, or a handful of stars.

I let my first kaleidoscope get away. When I was nine, my family visited Corning Glass Works in upstate New York. The factory was full of amazing objects made of glass. In the gift shop I saw a pretty kaleidoscope, but I chose another souvenir instead. As soon as we drove away, I regretted my choice. I never forgot that kaleidoscope.

Back home, I leafed through a 1917 edition of the children's encyclopedia *The Book of Knowledge*, where I saw some instructions for a project called "A kaleidoscope a boy can make." *Of course*, I thought, *a girl could make one, too*, and so I did. I was hooked! That project led me to collect kaleidoscopes and learn about them. I invented more scopes of my own, figuring out how to make the picture in the tube brighter and livelier. Eventually I started my own business, creating and selling scopes. That was almost 40 years ago and I'm still excited about kaleidoscopes!

This book is a chance to share my excitement, to show you what kaleidoscopes can do, and to show you what you can do with kaleidoscopes. I wrote the first edition of this book in 1995. In the decades that have passed since then, the world has changed a lot. There were not nearly as many crafts resources then as there are today. Many things we take for granted now either didn't exist or were very new, like cell phones and the Internet. Today, resources are all around us. If we need a material to create a project, it might already be in the recycling bin. We can find inspiration for a design with just a few taps on the keyboard.

One thing that has not changed is people's love of kaleidoscopes. The magic of the ever-changing vision will never get old. Just as that trip when I was nine led me to my career as a kaleidoscope artist, perhaps something in this book will set you on a new path that will lead to something in your future. You can start your journey at the beginning and follow the book to the end, or you can flip through the projects in any order. There's no right or wrong way to go. Just an infinite world of surprises and knowledge ahead.

HOW TO USE THIS BOOK

Are you ready to begin your kaleidoscopic journey? Before you do, let's go on a tour of what you'll find within the pages of this book.

In Chapters 1 and 2, you'll learn the basics behind the history and science of kaleidoscopes. You'll find **experiments** along the way—they're included in boxes called "Try This!" and "Test It Out!"

Sometimes a project calls for the use of a sharp tool or a drill—and only an adult should handle these items. You'll find an **Ask a Grown-Up!** icon at the top of any experiment that requires the help of an adult.

The kit is full of awesome stuff—you might have already opened it to see what's in there! For more details on its contents, see page 38. Then, on page 40, you'll learn how to put together the **master kaleidoscope** in the kit.

Once you've mastered the inner workings of your new kaleidoscope, you can turn to the projects to check out the **Variations** (starting on page 48).

After you learn to trick out your master kaleidoscope, you'll be ready for the big leagues! Check out the **Recycled Projects**, starting on page 69, to learn how to make your own kaleidoscopes out of materials that can be found around the house.

You may want to refer to the **Techniques** section in the back of the book, starting on page 117, if you want to become a true expert and kaleidoscope master.

Check out the **Templates** (pages 113 to 116) for some original designs to trace, and for some tips on how to create your own kaleidoscopes out of everyday materials, see the **Resources** section on page 121.

CHAPTER ONE

KALEIDOSCOPE HISTORY

KALEIDOSCOPE HISTORY

We have Scottish scientist Sir David Brewster to thank for the invention of the kaleidoscope. Born in Edinburgh in 1781, he spent his life studying the principles of light and optics, and his hard work was rewarded by many discoveries. His designs for lighthouses, for instance, saved the lives of thousands of sailors. And there's even an angle named for him: Brewster's Angle.

Brewster was most interested in what happened when light was *reflected*, or bounced, off an object. None of his inventions brought him so much fame, or brought so much joy to others, as the kaleidoscope, which works because of light reflection.

However, the idea behind the kaleidoscope wasn't new, even in Brewster's day. Ptolemy, a Greek mathematician who lived almost 2,000 years ago, had written about a surprising thing that happened when two or more reflecting surfaces (like mirrors) came together.

What caught Ptolemy's eye was the multiplication of images—the same thing that makes a kaleidoscope work. An object in

front of one mirror will be reflected once. An object in front of two mirrors can be reflected four, five, six, seven, eight, or more times, depending on the angle between the two mirrors.

Brewster noticed that the patterns made by bouncing light could be impressive—even beautiful. So, in 1815, Brewster was inspired to add color and movement to the reflections revealed in his two mirrors. He put the mirrors in a tube, and added a clear box called an *object chamber* to one end. In the chamber, he trapped bits of colored broken glass, and then figured out a way to turn the chamber while it was still in the tube.

Brewster called the view inside the tube "a phenomenon which could be considered as one of the most beautiful in optics."

Brewster described his invention in his 174-page book, *The Treatise on the Kaleidoscope*. He explained how to build a scope, where to put the eyepiece, even how to choose the best color combinations. Compared to writing his book, building a model of the invention was easy—maybe too easy. The kaleidoscope was a roaring success, and more than 200,000 were sold within the first few months after Brewster filed his patent. Unfortunately for him, a mistake on his patent application meant that many were sold by companies that paid nothing for the use of his invention. Popular as it was, it earned him little money.

Still, Brewster was a practical man, and he hoped that the kaleidoscope could be a tool to help designers. It's true that kaleidoscopes have inspired beautiful designs for buildings, books, rugs, jewelry, and much more. But the world loved his invention as a toy to amuse children and adults.

To this day, kaleidoscopes are still amusing us, thanks to the seemingly limitless stunning patterns waiting to be seen in each scope. Brewster even argued that you will never, ever see the same pattern twice! That's why it can be hard when you are trying to share what you see inside a kaleidoscope with a friend. No matter how carefully you pass the scope, one bead might move

Brewster's original kaleidoscope

FUN FACT

Kaleidoscope

Sir David Brewster followed the fashion of his era in choosing a name for his invention. Educated people of the early 1800s were expected to know the ancient languages of Latin and Greek. So Brewster put together three Greek words: *kalos*, meaning "beautiful"; *eidos*, meaning "form"; and *skopeo*, meaning "to see." So, the word *kaleidoscope* means "I see a beautiful form."

and the whole image could change. (Just wait until we address that problem in the Double Take project on page 97.) One thing's for certain, though—the ever-changing pattern doesn't get boring!

FUN FACT

Brewster's Less Famous Invention

Sir David invented another optical toy that became quite popular in Victorian homes: the lens-based *stereoscope* (also called a *stereopticon*). Unlike the kaleidoscope, which remains popular today, stereoscopes are now found primarily in antiques shops. (Look at the stereoscope below—it does look pretty ancient, doesn't it?)

Here's how it worked: The stereoscope used a viewer to transmit an image from a pair of nearly identical photos on a card. People were able to look at the picture cards and see views of the world that made it seem as though they were there—a fun diversion in a time without movies or TV.

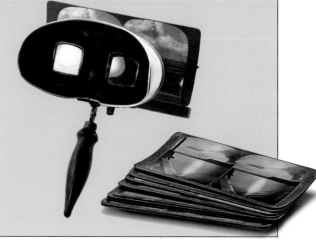

ARE YOU SEEING THINGS?

Look at the hexagon on this page. Close one eye and hold up one finger about six inches from your face, so that it covers the hexagon. Hold still. Now switch—close the first eye and open the other one. Did the design jump back into view? Try again with your finger even closer to your face. The design will appear to move even farther.

We are aware that our eyes see objects from different positions—after all, they're in different places on our head. Similarly, a stereoscope (opposite) uses special lenses. They bend the light coming from the two photos to your two eyes, and then the brain combines the separate photos into one image, creating the illusion of depth. A scientist named Euclid discovered this type of

vision, also called *binocular vision*, way back in ancient Greece. Have you ever looked at a bird through a pair of binoculars? The binoculars help your two eyes magnify the view of a faraway object with two lenses.

3-D GLASSES

Have you been to a 3-D movie? Did you feel transported? That's the way people looking through Brewster's stereoscope (see page 6) felt. They went on adventures and saw distant parts of the world, all while staying in one place. Now you can make your own pair of 3-D glasses to take on your own adventures!

YOU WILL NEED:
- Scissors
- 1 small piece of cardstock (at least 5½" x 3")
- Pencil
- Ruler
- Red and blue cellophane (from your kit)
- Clear tape

❶ Use the scissors to cut the cardstock into a 5½" x 3" rectangle. Fold it in half widthwise.

❷ Make a mark with the pencil, about 2" from the top of the fold. Cut a triangular hole for your nose from that mark to the bottom of the rectangle.

❸ Unfold the rectangle. Fold the left side over to meet the middle crease. Draw a triangle with 1" sides, using the folded edge as the base of the triangle. Cut out the triangle,

and unfold the rectangle. You will have one diamond-shaped hole for your eye. Repeat with the other side.

❹ Cut a 1" square from the red cellophane and another 1" square from the blue cellophane. Tape the red square over the left eyehole and the blue square over the right eyehole.

❺ Look at the image below without your glasses. Then hold the glasses in front of your eyes and look again. The image should jump right out at you!

❻ Use your glasses everywhere you can! Take them to the movies or to look at 3-D pictures on the Internet.

"Look at me! I'm in 3-D!"

CHAPTER TWO

KALEIDOSCOPE SCIENCE

LIGHT

It can be hard to imagine life without computers, electricity, TV, the Internet, cameras—even the scanner at the checkout counter. Every one of those things is possible because people have learned to harness and control the energy of light. Light can be stretched, shortened, expanded, made stronger or weaker, or turned on and off. We now know that we can harvest the power of the most powerful light there is—the sun—and use that solar energy to light our world.

When you look into your kaleidoscope, you're not really seeing beads or marbles or other shapes. What you're really seeing is *light*.

Light is so much a part of our world that we usually take it for granted. That doesn't make it any less important—or any less mysterious. All vision depends on it. It acts in ways we might never imagine, even though it surrounds us all our lives and we see it every day.

The way light behaves is crucial to the workings of a kaleidoscope. In fact, it's essential to the way we see everything in the world.

Reflecting on the Nature of Light

For as long as people have been thinking scientifically about light, they have been wondering how it really works. Does it move in a flow like the ripples of water in a pond? Or is it like a bunch of little balls tossed off in all directions from its source? Scientists ask the question this way: Is light made up of waves or of particles?

The answer is both! Depending on what

experiments we try, light can behave like the waves in water or like zillions of tiny packets of energy, or like both at the same time.

As we learn about how kaleidoscopes work, one important thing to know is that light bounces. We call this bouncing effect *reflection*. Without reflection, kaleidoscopes would not work. In fact, without reflection we couldn't see anything unless it was *luminous* (see below)—giving off light of its own, like the sun or a lightbulb.

Here's how reflection works: Whenever light hits a surface, some of it gets soaked up, or absorbed, and its energy makes the surface warmer. (You've felt this when you've touched a dark-colored object that's been left in the sun or when you've walked on a hot sandy beach.)

But many of the light waves hit the object and *don't* get absorbed—they get reflected. When light hits an object straight on, it bounces straight off (if the surface is perfectly smooth and flat). If the light hits at an angle, it elbows off at the same angle.

Reflected light is what we see when we look at any object that doesn't shine with its own light. Sunshine bounces off a tree, a car, your dog, or this page, and some of that light reaches your eye. The sensors inside the eye send a message to your brain, which puts together a picture based on the message.

Light's Magical Properties

You might have seen a cartoon version of a mirage: After days in the desert, a thirsty traveler sees a beautiful oasis. But as soon as he reaches it, it disappears.

Sometimes people really are fooled by mirages. Light bouncing from visible objects high above the ground—such as treetops, clouds, and other parts of the sky—is bent when it passes from a layer of cool air high in the atmosphere to a hotter layer at ground level. This bending of light is called

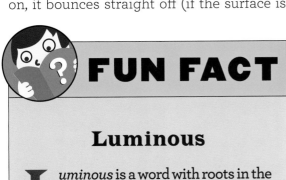

FUN FACT

Luminous

Luminous is a word with roots in the past. It's in the same word family as "light," which is *lumen* in Latin.

Cool Air

Hot Surface

Mirage

refraction—it happens when light passes from one medium to another.

The image looks to us as if we are seeing an upside-down tree, a cloud, and a patch of sky on the desert floor—because we believe we're seeing light coming into our eyes in a straight line. The real blue of the refracted sky looks like a lake. The tree and cloud seem to be reflected in the lake.

TRY THIS!

CHECK YOUR REFLECTION

You can use a simple piece of paper to demonstrate reflection. In the illustration, light waves coming from a lightbulb bounce, or reflect, off the angled white card onto the girl's face. Holding the card at a different angle aims the reflected light elsewhere.

Try it yourself. In your house, stand in front of a mirror under a light source that does not move, like the light fixture in your bathroom. Hold a piece of white cardboard under your chin. Look in the mirror as you move the cardboard in different directions. You will see that the light reflects onto your face at different places. Using this same principle, photographers sometimes use reflective objects to bounce light onto the people they're photographing.

REFRACTION IN ACTION

Reflection is just one of the surprising examples of the way light moves through our world. This experiment will show you another way light behaves, and you can do it in your own kitchen.

YOU WILL NEED:

- Teacup
- Quarter
- Assistant
- Pitcher of water

❶ Put the cup on the table and then put the quarter in the cup. Move so that you can still see the inside rim of the cup, but you can't see the quarter at the bottom.

❷ Stay standing next to the cup and have your assistant slowly pour in the water—don't move your head.

❸ As the cup fills, the quarter will come into view.

Did the quarter float to the top? Of course not—it's too heavy! If your assistant poured slowly enough, it shouldn't have even moved. So why can you see it now?

Sometimes the light that reaches your eye hasn't traveled along a straight path. Light can be bent when it passes from one substance to another. In this experiment, it traveled from the air to the water and back again. As you learned on pages 11–12, this bending is called *refraction*.

When you looked into the empty cup you were seeing only the light from the cup's inside wall. As water was added, it bent the light bouncing off the bottom of the cup (where the quarter was) until the light was bent at an angle that could meet your eye.

OPTICS

Have you ever noticed a drop of water on a leaf? The water magnifies the texture of the leaf, acting like a tiny lens.

Light can be bent by anything it passes through—a bottle of apple juice, a glass of water, hot air rising from a road in summer, a marble. One of the best tools for bending light is a *lens*—it's made for that very job. When light enters the lens, it bends. Lenses are specially shaped to bend light in a certain direction.

Outward-bulging lenses—thick in the middle and thinner around the edges—are called *convex lenses*. They bend light toward the center of the lens. Somewhere behind every convex lens is a place where those rays of light come together, called the *focal point*.

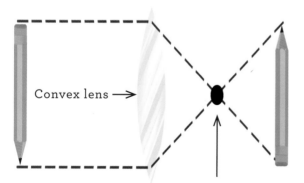

Convex lens →

Focal point

FUN FACT

Lens

The word *lens* comes from a Latin root. Originally it meant "lentil." A lentil is a small, round bean that is thin around the edge and thick in the center—the same shape as a convex lens.

FLIPPING OUT

The magnifying glass is one of the oldest optical devices ever made. It dates back to the ancient Egyptians, who used polished pieces of crystal to see small objects. Imagine suddenly being able to see things clearly that had always been a blur. It was the hi-def of the day!

Today, we have all sorts of optical devices to help us see better. But a magnifying glass can still be used to discover fun things—you can even do a flip without your feet ever leaving the floor! Here's how: Hold a magnifying glass at arm's length and stand in front of a mirror. As you look through the magnifying lens, back away from the mirror until you see yourself upside down! Or hold the magnifying glass at arm's length and look at the picture on this page. Back away from the image until it flips.

Like a magnifying glass, any curved glass will change the direction of light, sometimes with surprising results. To see an example, look at a friend through a large, clear glass of water. Your friend's face will appear enlarged, reversed, or misshapen. It might even disappear, depending on the way the light is bent.

Your Personal Lenses

You carry a pair of convex lenses around with you all the time. And what do you think those are? That's right. The lenses of your eyes.

These lenses, called *corneas*, make it possible for you to see clearly. At the back of your eye is the *retina*, a sensitive membrane covered in special cells that receive light and convert it into messages your brain can understand.

The cornea works the same way other lenses do: It bends the light that passes through it. If you have perfect vision, your cornea aims the images so that they fall right on your retina. If you need to wear glasses or contacts, it means your cornea isn't aiming the images in the right spot. So you need another lens between your cornea and the things you see. Glasses or contact lenses bend the light before it gets to your cornea. When the light reaches your eye, your cornea bends it a second time, and the image lands on your retina, right where it belongs.

However, with or without glasses, the image formed on your retina is always upside down. So why doesn't everything look like you're standing on your head? The reason is that your brain is programmed to interpret upside-down images as right side up. The world looks right to you because your brain is so good at understanding it.

If the focus of the cornea falls short of the back of the eye, a person is nearsighted and can't see faraway things well. If the focus is behind the eye, as in this illustration, the person is farsighted and has trouble focusing on things that are close up.

FUN FACT

The light-bending ability of the lens is based on its *focal length*, or the distance from the lens to the focal point. If the focal length is shorter, then the lens has a greater ability to bend light. If the focal length is longer, then less light is refracted by the lens.

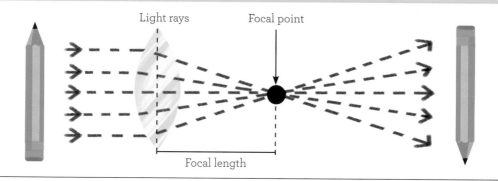

Light rays   Focal point

Focal length

MIRRORS

Take a minute to examine the mirrors that came in your kit. The surfaces are *very* smooth. That smoothness is what makes them good mirrors.

The more uneven a surface is, the more it scatters reflected light. Most objects have fairly rough surfaces—even a page in this book is considered rough—so that light hops off in lots of directions. However, we still get enough reflected light from the objects to be able to see them.

A mirror is different. Because it is extremely smooth, it reflects almost all the light that touches it, without much scattering. (Other smooth surfaces, such as a shiny button, work the same way.) The light bounces off the mirror in the same pattern as it came in from the objects. As a result, you don't see the surface of the mirror so much as you see the reflection in the mirror.

The picture that you see in the mirror is called the *virtual image*. When you look into a mirror, everything you see inside it looks just as "deep" as it is in the real world on your side of the glass. If you stand 5 feet away from the mirror, your reflection appears to be 10 feet away from you—that is, 5 feet *into* the mirror.

FUN FACT

Mirror

The dictionary defines a mirror as a polished or smooth surface that forms images by reflection. The word *mirror* comes from the Latin word *mirari*, which means "to wonder at."

MIRROR WRITING

That reflection staring right back at you in the mirror—it looks just like you, doesn't it?

Well, not exactly. Wink at it. If you shut just your left eye, the reflection stubbornly closes its right. Hold up your watch—the second hand on the reflection's watch moves backward! Put on a T-shirt with your favorite slogan or sports team, and the lettering or logo on the reflection's shirt is reversed.

But you can have the last laugh. Write the sound of a jolly chuckle—"OHO"—on a piece of paper in big letters. Now hold it up for the reflection to see. The paper in the reflection's hand still reads "OHO"! That's because the word is *symmetrical*: the same on the left of its center as on the right (see page 29 for more on symmetry).

For mirror writing to work, all the letters must be symmetrical from left to right (you can use A, H, I, M, O, T, U, V, W, X, and Y). And

that's not all! The letters *and* the words have to be symmetrical—that means they must be spelled the same way forward and backward. The words TOT, HAH, and YAY will all work.

You can also use words spelled only with letters that are symmetrical from top to bottom—B, C, D, E, H, I, K, O, X, and Z. (The numbers 0, 1, 3, and 8 work, too.) Write a sentence using only these letters. If you hold the page upside down when you look in the mirror you'll still be able to read it as if it were right side up.

If you turn the mirror so it divides the word horizontally, this trick will still work. Make a list of all the words you can spell from letters that are both vertically and horizontally symmetrical.

Place the long edge of a small, unframed mirror or one of your kit mirrors on the word "OHO" to divide the letters down the middle.

TEST IT OUT!

MULTIPLY YOUR MONEY WITH MIRRORS

It's better than a bank! In this experiment, you'll learn how reflection can make you a pile of coins.

YOU WILL NEED:
- Masking tape
- 2 mirrors from your kit
- Dime or penny

1 Put two pieces of masking tape across the back of the mirrors so they won't flop around.

2 Stand the two mirrors at a 90-degree angle from each other on their short ends. Put a shiny dime in the corner, head side up. Now you'll see four dimes.

3 Look closely at the reflections. The word *LIBERTY* reads "YTREBIL." Look at the reflection of the dime that's formed across the corner between the two mirrors. It's upside down compared to the original design but it reads just like the original: "LIBERTY." Why? Because the dime in the corner is not a direct reflection. It's a reflection of a reflection. The image is a *reversed reflection* of the first reversed reflection, so it looks like it is back to normal. In other words: a mirror image of a mirrored image.

4 Now change the angle of the mirrors to 60 degrees, so that you see six complete dimes in a circle. Keep changing the angle between the mirrors to make more or fewer dimes.

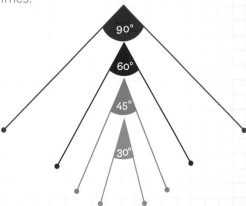

Position your mirrors over these lines to experiment with different angles.

Making Mirrors

Imagine some early humans foraging for food near a lake. They approach the lake's surface and look down—to see themselves! What do you think went through their minds? They might have thought it was magic, but in reality, they were looking in nature's mirror. If the water was completely still, the reflected image would have been just like a mirror's, but the slightest ripple of the water could have distorted that reflection.

The secret of mirror-making is thousands of years old. The first mirrors were made from plates of polished metal or stone. But much like ripples are unavoidable in water, it was hard to make those mirrors smooth. In the 13th century, when glassmakers learned how to coat the back of glass with tin or lead, bubbles and waves in the glass distorted the image on the mirror's surface.

To understand the difference between a perfect reflection from a flat mirror and a distorted reflection, think about a circus fun house mirror or a gazing ball. A gazing ball is a shiny, mirrored ball you might see in someone's garden. Because the surface is curved and not flat, the image is also curved.

Better mirrors came along with the development of *plate glass*—large, flat sheets of glass—with good reflective backing. The process of making this backing is called *silvering* or *foiling*.

With a regular plate-glass mirror—like one that you might have in your home—there is a coating of foil on one side of the glass. From the back this usually looks gray and opaque, but from the front it's silver. The light must first pass through the depth of the glass before it is reflected. Light is bent—or *refracted*—by the glass, so the viewer doesn't get a completely true image.

A top-coated, or *first-surface*, mirror has the reflective coating right on the top. The light does not have to pass through the glass at all, so the reflection can "bounce" right from the surface. The light is not bent and the image is true. Ancient mirrors were actually first-surface mirrors, made of polished, solid metal.

FUN FACT

During Victorian times, these glass ornaments—sometimes called *gazing balls*—were known as *butler balls*. Butlers would use a butler ball in order to watch houseguests without their knowledge. It was the hidden camera of its day.

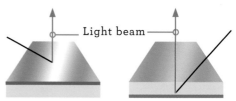

First-surface mirror   Regular mirror

First-surface mirrors are the best kind of mirrors for making kaleidoscopes. The plastics that I've suggested for the projects in this book will work as first-surface mirrors. The light will bounce off the top surface without passing through any depth.

Although a sheet of plain glass or clear polished plastic reflects some light, the addition of shiny foil or even black paper makes it far more reflective. Some of the earliest kaleidoscopes were made with pieces of glass coated with black paint.

TEST IT OUT!

ASK A GROWN-UP!

THE HALL OF MIRRORS

Have you ever been inside a hall of mirrors at a carnival? With this project, you can bring the carnival to your own house! It takes only two mirrors to make an endless parade of reflections.

YOU WILL NEED:
- Mirror on a wall (like the one over the bathroom sink)
- Adult
- Framed mirror

1 Stand in front of the wall mirror.

2 Have the adult hold up the framed mirror behind you facing the other mirror.

3 Look at the view in front of you—it's like a long tunnel of reflections.

As the light bounces back and forth between the mirrors, the images shrink down almost to nothing and become fainter with every

bounce. These images are called *converging reflections*, and they come with some surprising math built in. Each reflection is twice the size of the next one farther in. If you could stack them all up, they would be about twice as high as the tallest reflection.

The Reflections from Your Mirrors

Have you ever heard a magician's explanation of an illusion? They say, "It's all done with mirrors!"

Well, the magic in a kaleidoscope really *is* made with mirrors. It's the arrangement of mirrors inside a kaleidoscope that determines the image you see. Your master scope uses three mirrors. When you look through your eyepiece, you will be staring down a little triangular tunnel of mirrors at something called the object chamber (see page 39).

Inside your master scope, you will see a repeated pattern of triangles covering the whole viewing area. But one of those triangles will not be a reflection. You will be able to spot the real triangle because it will be brighter than the others. Also, if you hold the object chamber still and turn the barrel of the scope, it will be the triangle that doesn't move—all the other triangles seem to move around it.

A single mirror reflects one image: one "picture" of the object in front of it. You see that when you look in the mirror—there is only one you! You might think that two mirrors would reflect just two images, or that three mirrors would reflect three images, but this is not a case of simple addition. It's the arrangement of the mirrors inside a kaleidoscope that determines what the view will be like. Depending on the angle between the mirrors, you might see three reflections of an object. Or six. Or eight. If the mirrors are directly facing one another, an endless parade or "chorus line" of reflections can be seen. That's what you saw in the Hall of Mirrors experiment on page 21.

The repeated images are arranged in a pattern that we call *symmetrical*. That means one side perfectly balances the other. You'll learn about symmetry on page 29. Kaleidoscopes with three mirrors make an image that seems to expand into infinity because there are so many reflections of reflections. Have you ever tried on clothes in front of a three-way mirror? Sometimes three-way mirrors are made with hinges—so you can pull in the two outer sides to form an equilateral triangle (*equilateral* means that all three sides of the triangle are equal). If you did this, you would be inside a three-mirror kaleidoscope!

Polycentral

The Greek word *polus* means "many." Your master kaleidoscope has three mirrors. The symmetry in a three-mirror scope is called polycentral, meaning "having many centers."

COLOR

Just like light, the familiar colors of our world are more complicated than they seem. Wherever we look, the things we see are full of color. Or are they? Actually, most of the color we see is really another trick of light.

Think about some of the most colorful things you can imagine, such as paint, crayons, and jelly beans. The big surprise is that color doesn't exist in any of them!

Now think about a beam of light. You might say that it's white, wouldn't you? Well, here's another surprise: That white light is made up of every color in the rainbow.

Rainbows

The colors of the rainbow hide in plain sight all the time. The first scientist to realize this was Sir Isaac Newton, an Englishman who lived in the 1600s.

In an experiment, Newton passed white sunlight through a triangular glass shape called a *prism*. The light splintered into a pattern of pure colors—red, orange, yellow, green, blue, indigo, and violet, in that order. When people looked at this array of colors—called a *spectrum*—most assumed that something in the glass had changed the light to give it color. But Newton understood

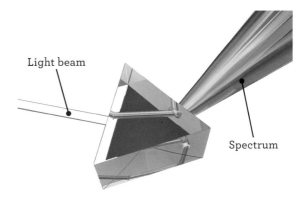

White light from the left side of this crystal is bent as it travels through the glass, creating a stream of spectrum colors.

that the prism had only separated the white light into colors that were there all along.

To understand this concept, think of light as a wave. Each color of light has a different size wave—some colors have small waves, so they use more waves to cover the same distance as other colors with larger waves. Another way of saying this is that the colors have different *wavelengths*.

Red light has longer wavelengths; violet light has shorter ones. The wavelengths of the other colors fall between these two. When these mixed wavelengths pass through a prism, the long waves of red light are bent the least. The shorter waves of violet light bend the most. All the colors bend at a different angle, and as they do, they separate. A spectrum is created.

What's Really on Your Paintbrush

Now that you've seen where color is, let's think about where it isn't. It *isn't* in a box of watercolor paints, despite what you might think.

What's really there is a selection of light-absorbing materials, called *pigments*, mixed with some other materials that help you apply the paint. When you use the paint, it seems as if you're just covering a surface with the color you've chosen. The substance that looks like the color in your paint box is just another example of light reflection.

Let's say you're painting a picture of the American flag on a piece of white paper. You start with the red stripes. You've put down pigment that soaks up every color in white light except red. The red light bounces off, and that's the color the stripes appear to be. When you paint the blue part of the flag, the paint appears blue because it reflects blue light and absorbs the other colors. The stars and the rest of the stripes are unpainted. Because they absorb *none* and reflect *all* the

THE COLOR WHEEL

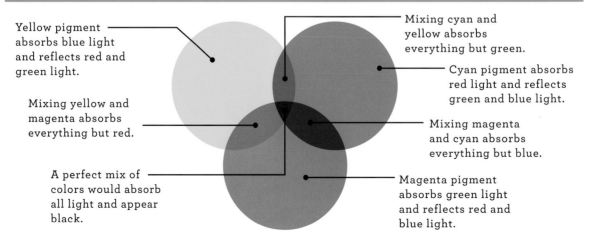

Yellow pigment absorbs blue light and reflects red and green light.

Mixing yellow and magenta absorbs everything but red.

A perfect mix of colors would absorb all light and appear black.

Mixing cyan and yellow absorbs everything but green.

Cyan pigment absorbs red light and reflects green and blue light.

Mixing magenta and cyan absorbs everything but blue.

Magenta pigment absorbs green light and reflects red and blue light.

CREATE YOUR OWN SPECTRUM

If you look carefully enough, a flash of spectrum colors can be seen in lots of places—a patch of oil floating on a wet driveway, on the surface of compact discs, or in soap bubbles. Whenever you see the spectrum, remember: The colors are really *in the light*.

You can create a spectrum with just a bucket of water and a simple reflective surface. The water works just like a prism, breaking up the white light.

YOU WILL NEED:
- Hand mirror that won't be damaged in water (don't use your kit mirrors)
- Bucket or deep dish filled with water
- Flashlight
- White wall or white piece of paper

❶ Set your mirror in the water at an angle.

❷ Move the flashlight beam around, aiming the flash of reflected light at a white wall or piece of paper.

❸ The spectrum should appear on the white surface, with the colors separated so that you can see them.

spectrum colors, they appear to be white.

If you try mixing your paints, you'll get combinations of pigments that absorb and reflect different colors. For instance, put yellow and blue pigments together and you'll get green. That's because the mixed pigments for those colors absorb all the wavelengths in white light *except* for those in the green range.

The color wheel at left shows how mixing pigments can make most of the colors in nature. Magenta, yellow, and cyan (also known as red, yellow, and blue) are basic

for this kind of color creation, so we call them the *primary colors*. Even though it all works by *adding* pigments—not colors—to *subtract* light.

Suppose you mixed all your pigments together. You'd get something that looks like dark mud. That mixture would have so many pigments that it would subtract almost all the visible wavelengths. If the absorption was perfect, your everything-but-the-kitchen-sink mixture would be black, reflecting no light at all.

Creating Filtered Light

Inside a kaleidoscope's object chamber, any object that doesn't transmit or absorb light reflects it. Objects that don't transmit light—*opaque* objects—show up as *silhouettes*, or dark outlines.

The kaleidoscope doesn't mix pigments, but it does give you a chance to look at another way color becomes visible.

When white light passes through a piece of colored cellophane like the pieces in your kit, the cellophane knocks out some of the colors. If you hold your red cellophane between a source of white light and a white piece of paper, you will see a red "shadow" on the piece of paper. The cellophane has blocked the other colors in white light, and red is all that is left to pass through and bounce off the paper to your eye.

When you put cellophane over the end of the object chamber, you subtract all the colors in white light except the color of the cellophane. Objects in the chamber will look like the color of the cellophane if they reflect or transmit light in those wavelengths—or they will look dark if they don't.

TYPES OF REFLECTED LIGHT

The toaster is *reflective*. Light from the juice and berries bounces straight back, giving us a clear image of breakfast.

The bagel is *opaque*. Light waves coming from the far side of the toaster cannot pass through.

The glass is *translucent*. Some light can pass through, so we can see the orange juice. But some of the light is blocked, so we also can see the surface of the glass.

The bowl is *transparent*. Almost all the light from the berries passes through and reaches our eyes.

THE WAVY ROPE EXPERIMENT

A simple experiment makes the wave-like behavior of light easier to imagine. Have a friend hold one end of a jump rope or a long piece of string. Gently shake your end of the rope while your friend holds the other end still. Watch to see a "wave" pass from you to your friend. If you move the rope up and down, you will see a wave that looks like the squiggle below. But you can make waves to the left and right, and at any other angle, depending on which way you move the rope. Light waves move in the same way—in any direction along the path they travel.

Now pass the rope through something that stops it from moving in all directions, such as through the back of a slatted chair. If you move the rope up and down, the waves still reach your friend. If you move the rope from side to side, they don't.

A polarizing filter does the same thing. At the beach, where light reflects off the sand and water, our eyes may get 10 times as much light as we need. This phenomenon is called *glare*, and a lot of it comes from light that vibrates in horizontal directions. By wearing sunglasses made with polarizing lenses (designed to allow only vertical vibrations to pass through), we shut out most of that painful glare, making it easier to see.

Polarized Light

Ordinary light vibrates in every direction. But *polarized* light vibrates only in *one* direction. It can thus create unusual effects in a kaleidoscope. To understand it, let's think again about the wave theory of light.

The squiggle on this page isn't a very good picture of a light wave. The vibrating particle that creates the wave isn't moving just up and down, as the squiggle would suggest. It moves in all directions.

This squiggle shows how light waves may travel in one direction.

 **TEST IT OUT!**

 ASK A GROWN-UP!

POLAR VISION

I f you can find an old, discarded pair of plastic polarized sunglasses in your house, you can use them to see how effective they are at blocking light.

YOU WILL NEED:

- Pair of plastic polarized sunglasses that can be taken apart—the kind you'd get at a 3-D movie work well

❶ Ask an adult to take the lenses out of the sunglass frames.

❷ In each hand, hold one lens by its edge.

❸ Hold both lenses in front of your eye—one on top of the other—so you can look through both at the same time.

❹ Slowly twist one hand so that one lens rotates while the other lens remains still.

You'll see the view change drastically. In one position, there should be plenty of light coming through; in another, almost none.

When you see light through the lenses, the polarizing filters are lined up in the same direction. The "slots" in both filters run the same way, so they'll allow light through. But when you turn the first filter 90 degrees (a quarter of the way around), the second filter stops all the light that came through the first one. Then you can't see anything.

SYMMETRY

When you tried Mirror Writing (page 18), it worked because of *symmetry*. When you look into a kaleidoscope, the image you see is symmetrical. An amazing number of objects in nature, science, architecture, and art are symmetrical. The view inside your kaleidoscope is symmetrical because opposite parts of the view balance each other. Symmetry is the balance we see in the construction or arrangement of things.

Plane and Simple

The human body is an example of natural symmetry. Think about it while you look at yourself in a mirror. You'll see a pair of eyes, ears, arms, hands, legs, and feet. If you could see inside your body, you would notice that your brain is divided into two halves, called *hemispheres*. You have two lungs and two kidneys that are symmetrical, too.

Lay your hands, palm down, on a flat surface. They're not exactly alike, are they? Your left hand has a thumb to the right, with the pinkie on the left. Your right hand? It's the reverse.

This symmetry is like the symmetry between a real object and its mirror image in the kaleidoscope. To prove this to yourself, try placing just your left hand on the table. Set up a mirror next to it. You'll see that the reflected hand looks very much like your right hand.

The surface of the mirror is like a wall between your hand and its reflection. The symmetry between the hand and the image balances along that make-believe wall. This is called *plane symmetry, line symmetry,* or *bilateral symmetry*. It has nothing to do with planes that fly in the sky (although those planes appear to be symmetrical from some angles). A plane can also be a flat surface.

In the Mirror Writing experiment (page 18), we used the symmetry of the alphabet to help us write some words that we could read both ways in the mirror. Look at the alphabet again. Can you spot the letters that have plane symmetry? Some letters are symmetrical from top to bottom—vertically—and some from side to side—horizontally. Only nine letters of the English alphabet show no plane symmetry. Can you pick out which letters those are?

Now take a look around the room. Do you see any examples of plane symmetry? Maybe a table, a desk, a clock, or a piece of fruit? There are examples of plane symmetry everywhere!

Nature's Symmetry

Butterflies and humans aren't the only living things that have symmetry. Many sea creatures have twin shells that open and shut like the two covers of a book. The plant world also has countless examples of symmetry. Imagine a leaf: It can be divided into two identical halves (that's mirror-image symmetry).

Look at the sea star pictured here. It doesn't have *plane* symmetry like a leaf, but it does have another kind of symmetry. The sea star's patterns rotate around a center point. This kind of symmetry is called *radial symmetry*—it's the same kind as the symmetry we see reflected inside a kaleidoscope. Microscopic sea plants called *diatoms* have radial symmetry, like the spokes of a wheel. The design looks delicate but is really very strong. The most beautiful diatoms look like the stained-glass "rose" windows in great churches.

Crystals are another part of the natural world rich in symmetry. A snowflake is an ice crystal with a complicated structure so tiny you may not be able to see it. Each snowflake begins with molecules of water high in the atmosphere. Because each water molecule has three atoms—two of hydrogen and one of oxygen—it forms a triangle with three equal sides.

As the water molecule turns to ice, the triangular molecules attach to one another and rearrange themselves to form hexagons—the shape of an ice crystal. As the crystal falls through the air, each side becomes the framework for more growth. By the time a snowflake reaches the ground, any number of elaborate forms may have taken shape. The lacy designs we know as snowflakes are infinite—just like the image in your kaleidoscope! And just like every single snowflake is different from the next, each turn of your scope gives you an image that is different from the last.

TEST IT OUT!

DISCOVER PLANE SYMMETRY IN NATURE

Think of all the beautiful butterflies you have seen. Did you know that a butterfly is a great illustration of plane symmetry? Let's make one fly!

YOU WILL NEED:
- Tracing paper
- Pencil
- Scissors
- Markers
- Pipe cleaner with a chenille stem
- Clear tape
- Hand mirror

❶ Trace the design below onto a piece of tracing paper.

❷ Use scissors to cut out the butterfly wing shape. Color in the wing with bright markers.

❸ Make a crease along the fold line to create a little flap.

❹ Cut a small piece of pipe cleaner to make the butterfly's antennae. Tape the antennae to the butterfly's head.

❺ Tape the flap to the mirror, so that it's under the butterfly wing. Now the butterfly half has grown into a whole butterfly! Wave the mirror gently around and up and down, and watch the butterfly fly.

What other things can you draw half of? An airplane? A boat? A car? Just make a little flap at the bottom of your drawing so you can tape it to the mirror.

FLAP

TEST IT OUT!

UNMELTABLE SNOWFLAKES

A true snowflake is a six-sided structure. Maybe you have cut paper to make snowflakes in school. But I bet you weren't thinking too much about how those paper creations related to a kaleidoscope. Just as you never see the same snowflake twice, you will never see the same thing in your kaleidoscope twice. As you fold the paper in this project, you will also be unlocking a few secrets of geometry.

YOU WILL NEED:
- Paper
- Scissors

❶ Fold a square piece of paper in half.

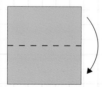

❷ Fold it in half again. Unfold the paper once—you should have a rectangle with a crease in the middle.

❸ Fold the right edge of the paper into the middle crease. Unfold. Now you should have the middle crease and one crease in the middle of the right side of the rectangle.

❹ Fold the left uppermost point of the rectangle across the center fold to meet the bottom of the fold you just made in Step 3.

❺ Fold the right uppermost point over the left so that the folded edges meet. You should now have a triangle with two flaps at the bottom.

❻ Fold up the points at the bottom, as shown.

7 Flip it over. Now you should see an equilateral triangle! Fold the triangle in half.

8 With the scissors, cut the wide edge opposite the point at an angle, as shown.

9 Cut shapes into the folded edges. Be careful not to cut all the way across the triangle.

10 Unfold your snowflake!

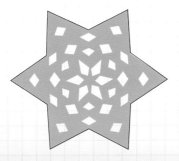

Man-made Symmetry

Whether animal, vegetable, or mineral, the list of living and natural things with some sort of symmetrical structure is almost endless. And humans have been mimicking nature's symmetry for years.

When people began to make things with their hands, whether useful objects for everyday living or works of art, they often made symmetry a part of the design. Sometimes the object or work of art was symmetrical just because it worked well that way. A skilled woodworker of long ago might have built a four-legged table—that's plane symmetry—because a table made that way is sturdy.

All over the world, since the beginning of history, human beings have used circular and geometric patterns as part of their symbolism in different art forms. Look up any of the following terms, and you'll be on your way to a fun research project:

- Huichol yarn paintings
- Persian carpets
- Amish quilts
- Millefiori paperweights
- *kippot*

- Japanese *temari*
- Tie-dye
- Mexican folk art (*ojos de dios*, or "God's eyes")
- Native American dream catchers
- Celtic art
- Ukranian *pysanky*

Circular designs like these can also be called *rosettes* or *medallions*. When you look into a kaleidoscope, you open a window into that same special way of seeing.

FUN FACT

Mandala

Mandala is a design made of various geometric shapes. In Hinduism and Buddhism, mandalas are symbols that represent the universe. They were, and still are, used to help people meditate. However, the word has become a term that can describe any pattern that represents the cosmos. In fact, many kaleidoscope artists use the word *mandala* to describe the inner vision in a kaleidoscope.

TEST IT OUT!

A ROSE WINDOW FOR YOUR WINDOW

Symmetrical forms have been used in cathedrals for thousands of years. Even though a rose window in a cathedral might look like an ocean plant to you and me, the artists who crafted these magnificent glass structures had never seen a diatom (see page 30). In this project, you won't need a microscope *or* a cathedral to make a piece of art that will channel the great rose windows created in the Middle Ages.

YOU WILL NEED:
- Drafting compass
- Scissors
- Black construction paper
- Piece of tracing paper (at least 4¾" x 5")
- Glue stick
- Colored permanent markers

❶ Use the drafting compass to draw a 4½" diameter circle on the black paper. Cut it out with scissors.

❷ Follow the directions for cutting out a snowflake on pages 32–33. Because the paper is round, it will look quite different than the snowflakes you made before.

❸ Attach the circle to the piece of tracing paper with the glue stick. Flatten it out and let it dry. Trim off any excess tracing paper.

❹ Using the markers, color the tracing paper that you can see peeking through the cutout. To keep the design kaleidoscopic, repeat the same color for the same parts of the design.

The tracing paper is translucent, so when you hold your creation up to the light, the colors will let light shine through like a real rose window.

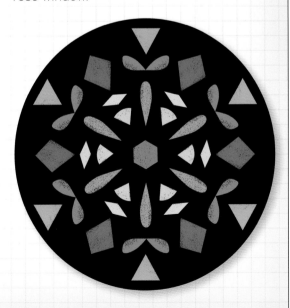

KALEIDOSCOPE PHOTO BOOTH

Check out your face in the mirror. Draw an imaginary line down the middle. Your face probably looks about the same on both sides, but chances are the left and right sides are a little different.

Want to prove it? You will need one of your kit mirrors and a picture of your face looking straight at the camera.

Put the edge of the mirror on top of the photograph, along the middle of your nose, so that it divides your face in half from the top of the head to the chin. Look first at one side of your face and the reflection of that side in the mirror. Now turn the mirror around and look at the other side of your face. It may look like it belongs to a different person. That's because the symmetry between the two halves of a real face is often close, but not exact. When you use the mirror in this way, the reflection makes each side of the face exactly symmetrical.

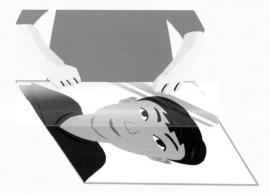

Right side

Original

Left side

CHAPTER THREE

YOUR MASTER
KALEIDOSCOPE

YOUR MASTER KALEIDOSCOPE

Once you make your own kaleidoscope, you will really understand what Sir David Brewster and millions of people find so much fun. This chapter will teach you how to assemble your master kaleidoscope—the one that came with this book—so that you can begin to look at the world in new ways. You'll also learn the types of kaleidoscopes, as well as what materials to keep in your artist's studio, so that you can be prepared to reach your full potential as a kaleidoscope artist in the next chapter.

CARDBOARD RING

IMPORTANT! It is possible to choke on small objects like the beads that came in your kit, as well as other items that you may be asked to use in a scope project. *Never* put anything from your collection in your mouth, and don't let anyone else (alert to little brothers and sisters!) do so either.

PING-PONG BALL   **CELLOPHANE**

THE OBJECT CHAMBER:
The short tube that will form the turning end of your kaleidoscope. This chamber holds the goodies that you look at through the eyepiece.

THE END CAP:
The frosted, flexible plastic cap to hold in the goodies.

LARGE CLEAR PLASTIC CIRCLE:
This piece will keep the mirrors in place.

THE EYEGUARD:
A small circle of clear plastic. This piece protects your eye!

THE BODY OF THE KALEIDOSCOPE:
The long tube is the scope body. It has a disk with a hole in the center fitted into the eyepiece end. (If your scope's disk is loose in the tube or package, insert it now.)

EYEPIECE

THE MIRRORS:
Three long rectangles of shiny plastic. Handle them by the edges only. Every fingerprint or smudge on their reflective surfaces will cause them to reflect less light.

THE GOODIES:
A starter set of beads, gems, and other objects to use in your scope.

Assembling Your Kaleidoscope

This page contains the official instructions for putting together your master kaleidoscope! To begin, clear a work space on a table or a counter, and spread out the parts for your master kaleidoscope (pictured at right). As you follow the instructions to assemble your master kaleidoscope, the mirrors, tubes, and rings may seem to be a tight fit. This is intentional—it will give you a better image in the finished scope. In addition to the master kaleidoscope, your kit contains three squares of cellophane and a Ping-Pong ball. You won't need these to construct your master kaleidoscope, but they'll be useful in the projects and experiments in other parts of the book.

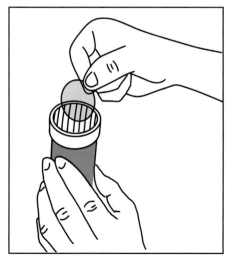

❶ Drop the eyeguard (the smaller plastic circle) into the long tube. The eyeguard should lie flat against the inside of the eyepiece—you may have to shake the tube a bit to get it into position. It should cover the hole in the eyepiece so nothing can fall into your eye. No matter what kind of scope you make, always make sure the eyeguard is in place before you look inside.

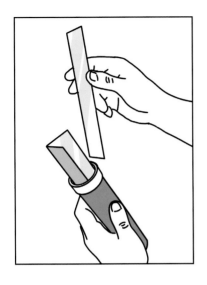

❷ Peel the protective film off the mirrors. Remember to handle them by the edges *only*. Form a V with two of the mirrors—make sure that the reflective surface is facing in—and carefully slide them into the tube. Carefully slide the third mirror into the tube to form a triangle with the other two mirrors. This is what we'll call a "three-mirror system."

Stop for a minute to look through the eyepiece. Wiggle your fingers at the other end. How many fingers do you see? Now turn the tube around and look through the open end. You should see a cluster of holes—multiplied reflections of the eyepiece.

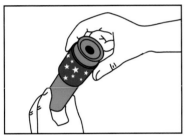

❸ Next, take the object chamber (the shorter tube) and slip it onto the scope starting at the eyepiece end. Slide it all the way up the tube until the outer ring attached to the tube stops the rolled edge of the object chamber.

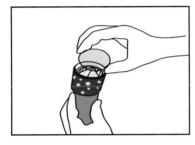

❹ Take the larger clear plastic circle and drop it into the open end of the object chamber. Then gently press it down.

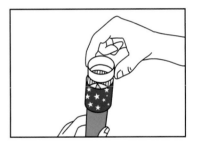

❺ Fit the cardboard ring into the open end of the object chamber to secure it in place.

❻ Now it's time for the goodies. Put as many beads and objects from your kit into the object chamber as you want. (Leave enough room for things to move around and for light to enter the chamber.) Then fit the end cap tightly over the object chamber to keep the goodies inside. Take a look!

VARIATION: MAKE A TELEIDOSCOPE

The only things you can put in an object chamber are things that fit. But what if size didn't matter? What if you could squeeze the whole world into a kaleidoscope? In this variation on the master scope, the world *is* your object chamber. You are making a *teleidoscope*. It's an entirely different instrument that also happened to be invented and named by good old Sir David Brewster. He called it a teleidoscope because the idea was to look through it at things far away. Just as a telescope helps you see the Moon and stars very far away, a teleidoscope changes the view of the landscape outside the tube.

❶ Take the end cap off your master scope and remove the goodies.

❷ Now you can point the tube at anything. The mirror system will break whatever object or landscape you choose into a series of reflections.

❸ Try looking at objects far away—the duplicated triangles are likely to look very different than the patch of direct light coming into your vision.

❹ Look at something very close up—the view will be like what you expect to see in a kaleidoscope. Each of the triangles will be very similar to one another in size and reflection. The image will be pleasing because it will have symmetry.

Look through your teleidoscope to see the world outside in beautiful symmetry.

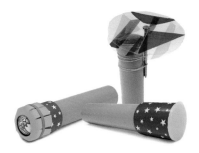

LEARN THE TYPES OF KALEIDOSCOPES

You are probably curious about making your own projects since you've just assembled your master kaleidoscope. And don't worry—you'll be making your own kaleidoscopes in no time. But first, it's important to understand the different types of scopes you can make.

There are five different types of kaleidoscopes. You may recognize some of them already—the master kaleidoscope, the one that you just assembled, is an example of a turning-chamber kaleidoscope. In the projects, you will explore all five types in depth, and with some variations.

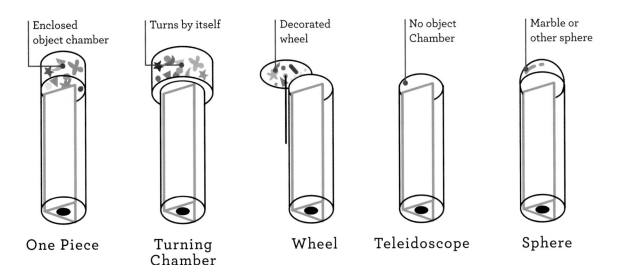

Enclosed object chamber	Turns by itself	Decorated wheel	No object Chamber	Marble or other sphere
One Piece	**Turning Chamber**	**Wheel**	**Teleidoscope**	**Sphere**

A KALEIDOSCOPE'S COMPONENTS

Now that you've learned the different types of kaleidoscopes, it's important to know that every scope is going to have (almost!) the same key features. Although there's a lot of room for variation within the world of kaleidoscopes, some things just have to be the same—for example, you'll have to have some kind of tube to look through, with mirrors in it to reflect your view. You can read more about these features in detail—and learn about the kinds of materials you can gather to make them—on page 121 in the Resources section. Your master kaleidoscope already has all of these elements in it, but in the recycled projects, you'll be making your own kaleidoscope components using repurposed tubes, bottles, and other kinds of recycled plastic. Read on for a short synopsis of the inner workings of a kaleidoscope.

The Kaleidoscope Body

The body of the kaleidoscope is the main piece that you see when you look at a scope—it houses the mirrors, eyepiece, and often the object chamber and end cap. It's usually a round tube—of any size—that will fit a three-mirror system (like the one that came with your master scope) in it. But wait! Your scope does not have to be round. You can make it square, rectangular, or triangular.

The Goodies

How would you describe the things we put inside a kaleidoscope? You could call them bits and pieces, objects, baubles, materials, treasures, gems, bling, things, stuff . . . but I like to call them *goodies*. Whatever you decide to name them, they will be used to create the final image in your scope. With goodies, the rule is: If it fits, it's fair game. Other than size, there is no limit to the kinds of goodies you can try in your kaleidoscope.

Eyepiece and Eyeguard

Your basic eyepiece is usually going to be a lid or a cap with a hole in the center. It fits over one end of the kaleidoscope body, so that you can look through the mirrors to the object chamber or wheel on the other side. The eyepiece should always be equipped with an eyeguard—a plastic piece covering the eyehole—so that nothing can accidentally fall through the kaleidoscope and hit you in the eye!

Mirrors

Mirrors are the key to your scope's image. But—although you can buy glass mirrors and have them cut specially to size—you don't have to use real mirrors in your kaleidoscope. Many other reflective materials are suitable for use in your scope. You'll learn to make several different types of mirror systems—

two-, three-, and even four-mirror systems—throughout the projects in this book. For a quick course on how to make a mirror system, simply turn to page 119 for a brief rundown on the technique.

Object Chamber

The short tube or container that will form the turning end of your kaleidoscope is called the object chamber. This chamber—which can vary in size and shape—holds the goodies that you'll be looking at through your mirror system. Because you need to see through it, your object chamber should always be clear.

End Cap

The end cap is what keeps the kaleidoscope's components in place. Usually (but not always), a kaleidoscope's end cap is translucent (frosted), so that light can enter the object chamber, but nothing beyond the chamber will be visible when you look through it. If a material is transparent (clear) and you want it to be translucent, you can sand it with a little piece of sandpaper.

End caps do not have to be able to snap onto the end of your tube—they can be flat pieces of recycled plastic that you tape in place. Just as long as it fits, you can use it!

Wheel and Axle

Sometimes, instead of an object chamber, your kaleidoscope will have a wheel (or two!) attached to the end of it with goodies glued or taped on. Like all wheels, this will need a post to turn on, called an axle. Often an unsharpened pencil that can be zip-tied onto your kaleidoscope body will work—along with a pushpin or clothespin

to keep the wheel attached to the axle. How big should the wheel be? Measure the diameter of your tube and double that number. The doubled number is the diameter of the smallest wheel you can use. (If the wheel doesn't cover the whole end of the scope, it's okay. You will see just a bit of the world beyond it.)

HELPFUL MATERIALS TO HAVE AROUND YOUR STUDIO

It's nice to keep some basic craft tools and supplies in one place so you can make kaleidoscopes whenever you want. Here are some materials that could be useful to have on hand:

- Black and colored foam with and without adhesive backing
- Circle templates (see page 113)
- Drafting compass
- Flat cardboard (cereal boxes work well)
- Pencils with erasers
- Protractor
- Recyclable plastic
- Regular-size paper scissors
- Rubber bands
- Ruler with a metal edge

- Small cuticle scissors
- Scrapbook paper
- Scraps of wrapping paper
- Clear tape
- Duct tape
- Thumbtacks or pushpins
- Tracing paper
- Zip ties
- White glue

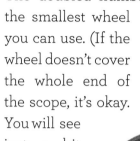

CHAPTER FOUR

THE PROJECTS

TXT ME Kaleidoscope

You can turn your master scope into a low-tech texting device. In this project, your message will always be in the vision—you can't miss it. For a really professional result, type the message on the computer and print it onto transparency film (available at office supply stores).

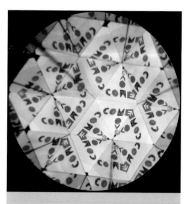

MATERIALS:

- Your master scope
- Piece of clear recycled plastic
- Thin permanent markers
- Scissors
- Clear tape

❶ Remove the end cap, the goodies, the cardboard ring, and the plastic circle from your master scope.

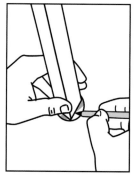

❷ Trace around the plastic circle onto the clear recycled plastic with a thin permanent marker. Trace an equilateral triangle (see page 113 for a template) inside the circle. Put the plastic circle back into the scope.

❸ Cut out the circle that you traced in Step 2. Write a message on it inside the triangle with permanent markers.

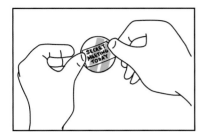

4 Cover the writing with a piece of clear tape to keep the message from getting scratched.

5 Place the message disk into the object chamber over the clear plastic circle. Replace the cardboard ring, and slide the object chamber back on the tube. Put the end cap back on.

6 Look through the eyepiece to read the secret message. Try turning the disk to rearrange the words—see how the pattern changes. Your message will always be visible as a pattern of your word backward and forward.

FUN FACT

Perimeter

The word *perimeter* comes from the Greek words *peri* (meaning "around") and *metron* (meaning "measure"). And it is just that—the measurement or distance around a flat (two-dimensional) shape. The perimeter determines the limits of the shape. Some people call it the border, margin, or outer edge. The perimeter of a circle is called the *circumference*.

VARIATION

Make a Mystery Message

To keep your message a bit of a mystery, you can jumble up the reflections by writing on recycled plastic *strips* instead of a circle. The strips should be small enough to tumble around in the chamber.

But why is the message so hard to read? Since the strip can fall outside the perimeter (see Fun Fact above) of the mirrors, sometimes only parts of it are reflected, making your original message seem more like a piece of a puzzle than a real message.

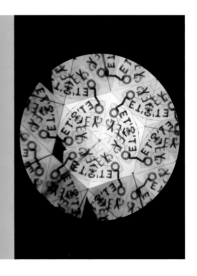

Scribble Scope

We have seen how words can look when they are "kaleidoscoped" in the TXT ME Kaleidoscope on pages 48–49. But what about works of art? Bring out your inner Picasso for this project and set free the artist in you! The simplest shapes or lines can be transformed into intricate patterns. Your "artwork" can be just a few scribbles, splashes of color, or a detailed drawing. Let your imagination run wild—you won't know what a drawing looks like inside a kaleidoscope until you try it.

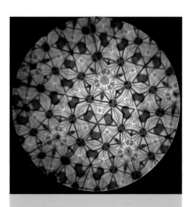

MATERIALS:

- Your master scope
- Thin permanent markers in a variety of colors
- Sheet of tracing paper
- Scissors

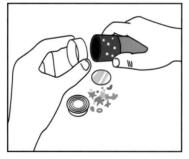

❶ Remove the end cap, the goodies, the cardboard ring, and the plastic circle from your master scope.

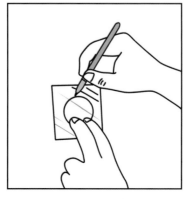

❷ Trace around the plastic circle onto the tracing paper with a thin permanent marker. Repeat to make as many circles as you want. Then put the plastic circle back into the scope.

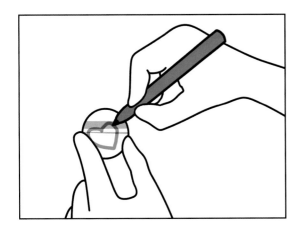

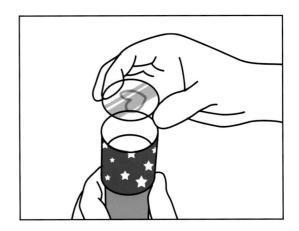

3 Using colored markers, draw pictures and designs on each of the tracing paper circles. Fill as much of each circle as possible with design and color. Cut out the shapes and fit one of them into the end cap. If the circle is too big, trim it a little so it fits.

4 Place the ring back into the chamber to hold the traced circle in place. Put on the end cap and take a look! When you're ready for a new view, switch out the tracing paper circle for another one.

Shadow Scope

If you look into your scope backward, what do you see? Oodles of little circles. What you are seeing is the light coming through the eyehole. You also see positive and negative space. Wherever the light has been blocked is the *negative space*. Everywhere you see one of the holes is the *positive space*. Working with this idea, we can turn your scope into a real show. In this project, we'll change the light coming into your scope chamber with a *shadow mask disk*.

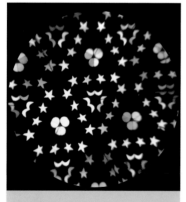

MATERIALS:

- Your master scope
- Pencil
- Black paper
- Scissors
- Assortment of hole punches (any shape)
- Assorted goodies

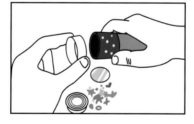

❶ Remove the end cap, the goodies, the cardboard ring, and the plastic circle from your master scope.

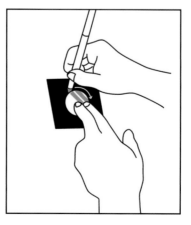

❷ Trace around the plastic circle onto the black paper with a pencil. Repeat to make as many circles as you want. Put the plastic circle back into the scope.

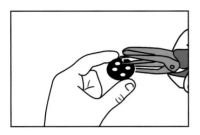

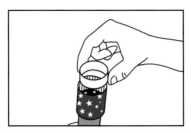

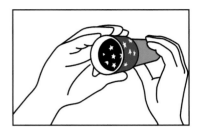

3 Cut out the black paper circles with the scissors. Punch holes or shapes into them.

4 Fit one circle into the bottom of the chamber, on top of the plastic circle. Then slide the ring back into the end of the scope.

5 Before filling the object chamber with goodies, look through the eyepiece and move the scope around the room as you would a teleidoscope (see page 42). You can see a shadow light show!

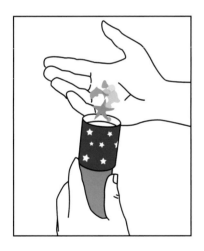

6 Now fill the object chamber with goodies and put the end cap back on. As you turn the chamber, the goodies inside will appear and then vanish within the kaleidoscopic image, framed by the shapes you have punched into the disk.

VARIATION

More Ways to Jazz Up a Shadow Mask Disk:

- Tape colored cellophane to one side of the shadow mask disk.

- Make a clear circle of recycled plastic the same size as the shadow mask disk. Scribble all over it with colored permanent markers. Stack the disks together in the chamber under the ring.

The Mirror Mask

Trick or treat! It may not be Halloween, but your scope can wear a mask whenever it wants. You'll want to try out lots of designs in this project, but remember—the objects you draw should all have plane symmetry (see page 29). Check out the Templates section (page 113) for more designs to try.

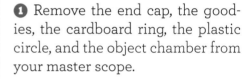

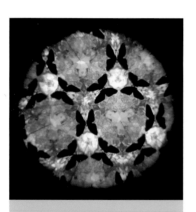

MATERIALS:
- Your master scope
- Sheet of clear transparency film
- Tracing paper and pencil
- Scissors
- Masking tape
- Printer paper (optional)

1 Remove the end cap, the goodies, the cardboard ring, the plastic circle, and the object chamber from your master scope.

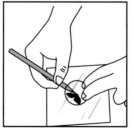

2 Trace the butterfly circle design (see opposite page) onto the clear transparency film with the tracing paper and pencil.

3 Cut out the butterfly circle. Place it on top of the mirrors in your kaleidoscope tube. Line up the edge of the butterfly half with the edge of one mirror. Use some small pieces of masking tape to keep the circle in place.

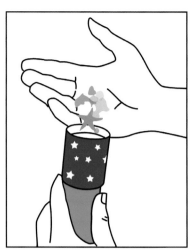
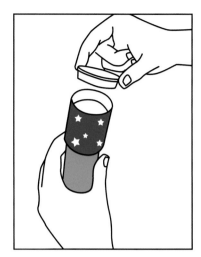

❹ Replace the object chamber, the plastic circle, the cardboard ring, the goodies, and the end cap. Take a look. What's all that fluttering? Each half made a whole butterfly, and each whole made a flock of flying, spinning butterflies. The colors of the goodies will tumble around behind the shapes.

❺ Repeat Steps 2 and 3 to try the other designs. Draw a few of your own in a circle that's the same size. Try looking at your designs without the goodies in the object chamber.

Ping-Pong Scope

A Ping-Pong ball, like the one that came in your kit, is a great thing to use in a kaleidoscope, because it's translucent—you can see light through it. If you doodle on it with thin permanent markers, it becomes a customized view that you've drawn just for you!

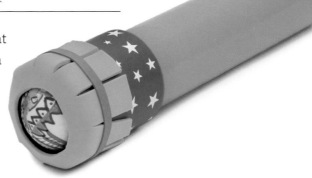

MATERIALS:

- Your master scope
- Foam strip with adhesive backing (1¼" x 5")
- Drafting compass
- Foam square *without* adhesive backing (6")
- Scissors
- Ping-Pong ball from your kit
- Colored permanent markers
- Rubber band

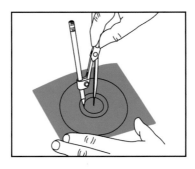

1 Remove the end cap, the goodies, and the cardboard ring from your master scope.

2 Curl the strip of adhesive foam with the protective paper facing in—so it fits inside the object chamber. The paper will help the ball move freely.

3 Using the compass, draw a 5" circle on the piece of nonstick foam. Keep the center point of your compass in the same place and draw a 1¾" circle inside the larger circle. Then draw a 1⅛" circle inside that.

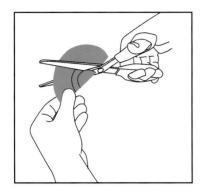

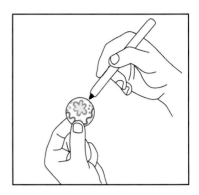

4 Cut out the largest circle and fold it in half so that you can still see the lines of the two smaller circles. Cut along the line for the smallest circle to create a 1⅛" hole in the middle of the foam.

5 Unfold the circle and cut notches from the outer rim to the remaining line that marks the 1¾" circle (the middle), as shown.

6 Draw colorful designs all over the surface of the Ping-Pong ball with the markers. Try out specific designs or just scribble lots of colors and swirls. Set the ball aside.

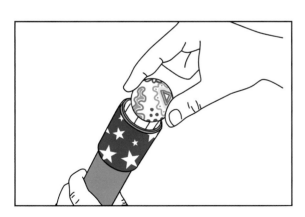

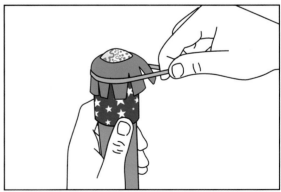

7 Put the Ping-Pong ball in the chamber and place the notched circle of foam over the end of the chamber so the ball can still be seen sticking through the hole.

8 Fold the flaps down against the tube and secure everything with a rubber band. Point the scope in the direction of a light source. As you look through the eyepiece, roll the ball around. It's a little like watching the earth spin!

Ocean Slow-Motion Scope

Have you ever opened your eyes underwater? Things look different: They float and drift in a graceful way. You can make a liquid-chamber scope that will create a floating view, just like the motion in the ocean. When you're choosing a plastic jar to hold the liquid, remember that it should be completely sealable, and it must also fit tightly into the open object chamber. Look for a plastic vitamin jar, clear spice jar, medicine jar, or other small, round, clear plastic jar. In the materials list, we'll just call for a spice jar, but know that any of these clear vessels will work here, and for any other project in this book that calls for a spice jar.

MATERIALS:

- Your master scope
- Spice jar with a tight lid (see headnote)
- Goodies that you don't mind getting wet, like seashells or beach glass (round are better than flat—the liquid will make flat objects stick to the inside of the jar)
- Water
- Colored duct tape
- Foam with adhesive backing (optional)

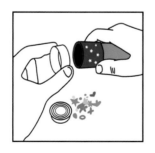

❶ Remove the end cap, the goodies, and the cardboard ring from your master scope.

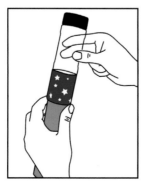

❷ Make sure the jar will fit securely into the open end of the object chamber. If the jar is too small or loose, wrap a strip or two of adhesive foam around the jar to make it snug. You don't want it to fall out as you are turning it. It's okay if the jar extends beyond the end of the chamber.

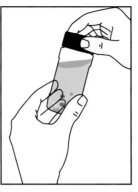
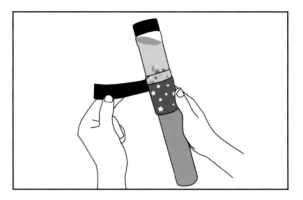

❸ Fill the jar a little past halfway with goodies. Fill it most of the way with water and tighten the lid of the jar.

❹ Push the jar into the chamber end of your scope. Secure it with a piece of tape. Now take the plunge—look into the eyepiece. When you're finished looking at your ocean scope, be sure to store any liquid-filled jars or containers standing up (with the lid at the top). You don't want any liquid to leak out.

VARIATION

Other Fun Things to Try in Your Liquid Chamber:

- Add a drop or two of food coloring to the water.
- Drop in a little dish soap and shake the jar to make some bubbles.
- Pour a little vegetable oil into the water. It is lighter than the water, so it separates into blobs, like a lava lamp! If you add some food coloring it will stain the water but not the oil.

The Revolutionary Turner

The object chamber in this scope is perpendicular to the mirrors—meaning, it's at a right (90°) angle in relationship to the body of the kaleidoscope. Because it's oriented in this way, you'll be turning the object chamber from the side. You may also want to turn the whole kaleidoscope tube as a unit to get the best movement for your view. Now get started and watch your scope flip out!

MATERIALS:

- Your master scope
- Clear, narrow spice jar (washed and dried completely)
- Assorted goodies to fit inside the jar
- 4 zip ties
- Scissors

❶ Remove everything except the mirrors from the inside of your master scope.

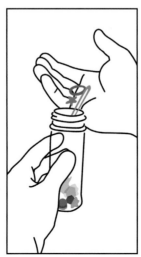

❷ Fill the clear jar at least halfway to the top with goodies. (If the jar has a wide mouth, this could be a good chance to use some of your larger goodies.)

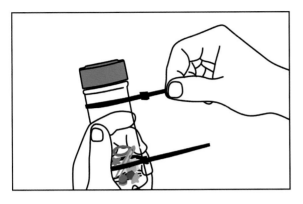

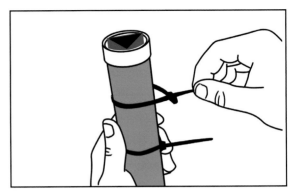

3 Secure two zip ties around the jar, pointing them both in the same direction. Pull the ties tight enough to hold the jar in place, but loosely enough so that the jar can turn freely. Leave the long ends of the ties dangling.

4 Place the other two ties around your master scope tube, about 2" apart.

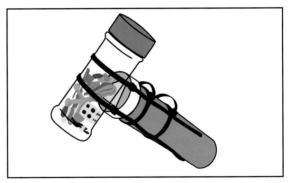

5 Position the jar opposite the tube's eyepiece so that its ties stretch down to the ends of the tube. Weave the jar's zip ties under the tube's zip ties. Pull the tube's zip ties tightly to secure the jar in place. Clip off any excess zip tie ends.

6 Twist the object chamber as you look inside to see what's in store. That's revolutionary!

Color Changing Scope

You read about polarizing filters earlier in "Polarized Light" (page 28). Now let's put that knowledge to good use. The effect that polarizing filters can have in your scope is something that words can hardly describe. The change in light levels is dramatic when it happens inside a kaleidoscope. When you're looking for your materials, note that not all sunglasses are made with polarizing filters. Some glasses may say UV protection but are not polarized. To be sure that you have the polarizing kind, hold one piece on top of the other. Then turn the top piece 90 degrees. If the place where the lenses cross each other gets darker (even turning black is okay), you have the right stuff.

MATERIALS:

- Scissors
- Assorted pieces of clear plastic (see Fun Fact)
- Drafting compass
- Lenses from a pair of 3-D glasses or polarized sunglasses (see headnote)
- Your master scope
- Masking tape

FUN FACT

Recyclers, rejoice! The kind of clear plastic you need for this object chamber is the kind we usually toss in the trash—a piece of clear cellophane from a wrapped candy, CD cases, clear tape (folded onto itself), packaging materials, or takeout containers. This plastic has a special quality. It has *birefringence*, or double refraction. The light passing through it is split in two directions, producing multiple spectrums. Almost every piece of plastic will produce a different range of colors.

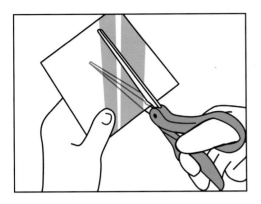

1 Use scissors to cut the assorted pieces of plastic into smaller pieces.

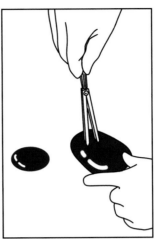

2 Use the drafting compass to draw two circles on the polarized plastic. Make one circle 1½" in diameter and the other 1⅝" in diameter. (The second size is the same size as the larger clear circle in your master scope.) Cut out the circles with scissors.

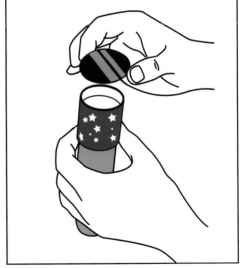

3 Remove the end cap, the cardboard ring, and plastic circle from your master scope. Fit the smaller polarized circle inside the tube, right on top of the mirrors.

4 Drop the plastic circle in place. Put the cardboard ring back into the scope. Fill the object chamber with the clear plastic pieces that you made in Step 1.

5 Fit the larger polarized circle into the end cap. Put the end cap back on the scope.

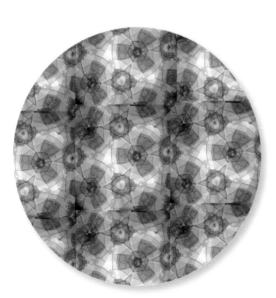

6 Take your Color Changing Scope to a sunny window. Turn the object chamber and watch the clear pieces change color!

Milky Way Scope

Treat yourself to a spiraling, out-of-this-world image—one that is very different from the geometric patterns we have been seeing. Filled with lots of light, this variation will look like a whirling new universe. It's practically a cosmic experience.

MATERIALS:

- Your master scope
- Piece of silver Mylar (about 5½" x 6½")

❶ Remove everything, including the mirrors, from your master scope.

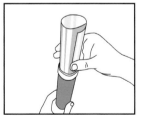

❷ Roll up the silver Mylar in a cylindrical shape and fit it inside the tube of your master scope. Let it spread out to line the inside of the tube.

❸ Put the object chamber back on. Look at the world swirl! Now add the plastic circle, the cardboard ring, the goodies, and the end cap back on. Take a peek: The image doesn't have any symmetry!

Color Wheel Scope

Let's make a color wheel to see how colors mix. Instead of painting an ordinary color wheel like you might create in art class, we'll discover how a revolving wheel of the primary colors (red, yellow, and blue) can make a rainbow of spectacular designs.

MATERIALS:

- Your master scope
- Ruler
- Scissors
- Two 5" squares of clear recycled plastic
- Cellophane from your kit
- Clear tape
- Pushpin
- Nail, at least 3" long
- 2 rubber bands

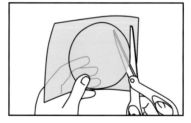

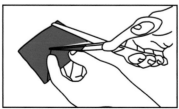

❶ Remove the end cap, the goodies, the cardboard ring, the plastic circle, and object chamber from your master scope so that you are holding just the long tube with the mirrors inside it.

❷ Cut out two circles, each 4½" in diameter, from the clear plastic.

❸ Cut a triangle of red cellophane that measures 2" on two sides and 3" on one side. Repeat with the blue and yellow cellophane. Tape the three triangles, as shown, on one of the clear plastic circles. The longest side of each triangle should be closest to the edge of the circle.

4 Cut a rectangular strip of each color of cellophane. Tape the strips to the other circle, as shown. Trim any edges that hang off the circle.

5 Ask an adult to help you punch a hole in the center of each plastic circle with a pushpin. Poke the nail through the holes to enlarge them.

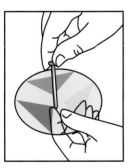

6 Arrange the disks back-to-back, untaped sides facing each other, to help them rotate more easily. Push them onto the nail all the way to the head of the nail.

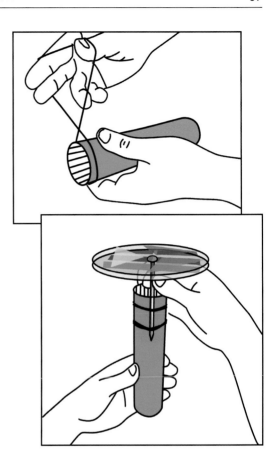

7 Wrap the rubber bands tightly around the long tube near the end of the cardboard ring. Lift up the rubber bands and push the nail under them. The sharp end of the nail should point toward the eyepiece, as shown.

8 Spin the wheels and watch the colors change!

Projecto Gizmo

Your master scope, a convex lens from a magnifying glass, a flashlight, and a dark room will help you turn your image inside out. That makes it easier to share the image with a friend.

MATERIALS:

- Your master scope
- Masking tape
- Magnifying glass (plastic works, but glass is better)
- Flashlight or another strong light source about the same diameter as the master scope (LED light is best)
- Dark room with a white wall or surface

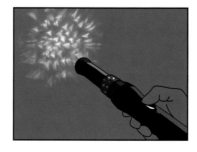

❶ Take the eyepiece and eyeguard out of your master scope. Tape the magnifying lens to the viewing end.

❷ Tape the flashlight to the end of the object chamber.

❸ Take your crazy contraption into a dark room. Turn on the flashlight and hold it about a foot from a white surface. Move the Projecto Gizmo back and forth until you find the place where it is focused best. The stronger the magnifying lens, the closer the focal point will be (and the closer you will have to stand to the white surface).

RECYCLED PROJECTS

The key to getting the best view in your homemade kaleidoscopes is having a good set of mirrors with straight edges. The mirrors that came in your master scope kit are great, but they aren't quite long enough to use in many of the scopes in this next section. So, you'll be learning how to make your own, with the help of an adult and some materials that can be found easily at a drugstore, hardware, or crafts store.

The best material for making a mirror is actually the stiff plastic that you can buy to frame posters. A sheet of poster frame plastic is usually big enough, so you'll be able to use it to make mirrors in many different sizes. If you ask an adult to cut lots of different sizes of rectangles from the poster plastic to match the mirror sizes in the projects, putting together your kaleidoscope creations will be a cinch! Here's the technique that an adult should use to cut the mirror material into rectangular panels with *very* straight edges.

ASK A GROWN-UP!

Score and Snap Technique

If you want to use a material that is too hard to cut with scissors or a paper cutter, here is an easier way to "cut" it into strips. After you have determined the width and length of your mirrors, the rest can be a *snap*.

MATERIALS:
- Box cutter and cutting mat
- Poster frame plastic
- Ruler with a metal edge

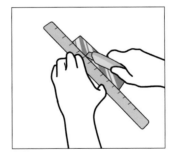

❶ Ask an adult to place a metal-edged ruler along the line you want to "cut."

❷ Have the adult run a box cutter or utility knife along the edge of the ruler, cutting into the material lightly several times. This will create a groove.

❸ Place the scored groove at the edge of a table and press down. The material should snap apart. If it doesn't, score the line a little deeper.

ASK A GROWN-UP!

Dippity Chip Scope

Here's an easy scope that you can make using an empty potato chip container. You can adapt these directions to any tube. The instructions below have measurements for a 3" x 9" can. If you find a can that's a different size, you can adjust according to the measurements that I used. You'll rely on the basic structure of this simple scope and mirror system to make many of the scopes in this chapter.

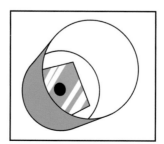

MATERIALS:

- 3" x 9" potato chip can (5¾ ounces) and lid, cleaned and dried completely
- Hammer and nail
- Scissors
- 2" square of clear, flat plastic
- 2 small rubber bands
- 3 strips of poster frame plastic (8¼" x 2⅜") (see page 69)
- Tape
- Sheet of black paper, the length of the tube
- 2¾" circle of clear, flat plastic
- Strip of foam with adhesive backing (½" x 9")
- Assorted goodies
- Printer paper and markers (optional)

❶ Ask an adult to punch a hole in the center of the metal end of the can with the hammer and nail. Press down the rough edges inside the can with the tip of the scissors.

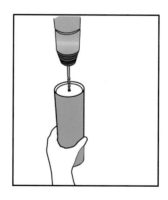

❷ Drop the 2" square of plastic into the can so it covers the eyehole. Make sure it covers the hole completely—this piece protects your eye!

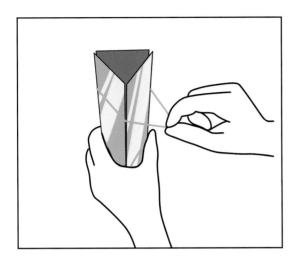

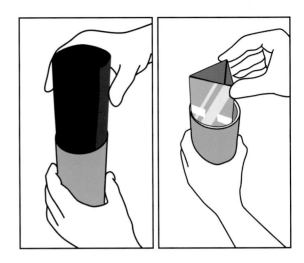

❸ Arrange the strips of poster frame plastic in a 3-D equilateral triangle—oriented just like your master scope mirrors. Slip the rubber bands over the ends to hold the triangle in place. Tape around the outside of the triangle to hold it together. Remove the rubber bands.

❹ Curl up the black paper and slip it inside the can. Slide the three-mirror system into the can. It should rest on the eyeguard that you inserted in Step 2.

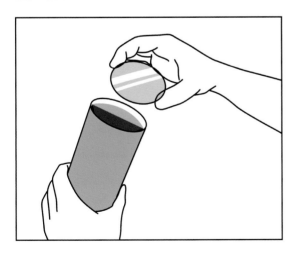

❺ Drop the plastic circle into the can, so that it rests on the mirror system. Peel the protective paper from the foam strip, and press the sticky side to the inside of the can, forming a collar that will hold the clear circle in place. The strip should be flush with the plastic circle—check to make sure that there are no gaps between the two. You have just created the object chamber of your kaleidoscope (yes, inside the can!).

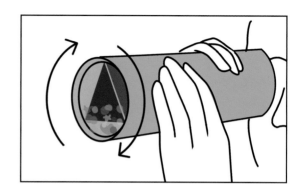

6 Now fit your goodies into the object chamber. Use the plastic can lid to close up the chamber. The lid is the perfect end cap—it's translucent, and it fits snugly on the can. You can take it on and off to try different assortments of objects in the chamber easily.

7 Look through the eyehole. Because the chamber is built right into the tube and doesn't turn independently, you'll have to turn the whole tube when you look through it.

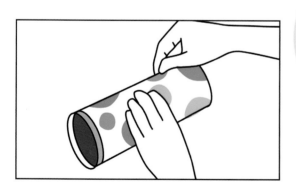

8 If you want to personalize your scope, decorate a standard sheet of printer paper with a marker—it will wrap nicely around the can.

ASK A GROWN-UP! Jr.

Cool Drink of Water

Drink up! The next time you guzzle a bottle of water, save the container. Not only will you be well hydrated, but you'll also be able to make a kaleidoscope that can quench your thirst for the creative and crafty. (Make sure you save the cap, too!) And, translucent food storage containers make great object chambers.

MATERIALS:

- Sturdy plastic water bottle, with the cap
- Ruler
- Paper
- Thin permanent marker
- Scissors
- Drill with ¼" bit
- 1" square of clear, flat plastic
- 1 or 2 sheets of foam
- 3 strips of clear poster plastic (about 1" wide, ¼" shorter than the bottle) (see page 69)
- An object chamber with the same diameter as the bottom of the bottle
- Sheet of black poster paper (about ¼" shorter than the bottle)
- 2 rubber bands
- Tape
- Assorted goodies

❶ Use paper as a straight edge to measure and mark a line around the outside of the bottle, about 1" from the bottom, with the thin permanent marker. Cut off the bottom piece with scissors.

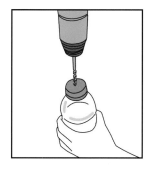

❷ Ask an adult to make a hole in the center of the plastic bottle cap with the drill.

❸ Drop the plastic square inside the cap so it covers the eyehole. Make sure it covers the hole completely—this piece protects your eye!

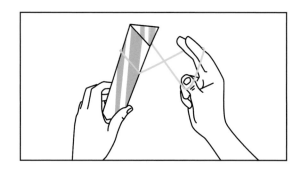

4 Trace around the bottle on the foam twice, to make two circles. Cut them out with scissors, cutting along the inside of the line so the circles will fit inside the bottle.

5 Arrange the strips of poster frame plastic in a 3-D equilateral triangle—oriented just like your master scope mirrors. Slip the rubber bands over the ends to hold the triangle in place. Tape around the outside of the triangle to hold it together. Remove the rubber bands.

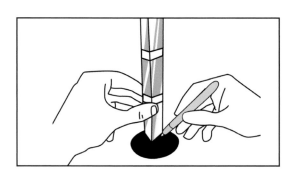

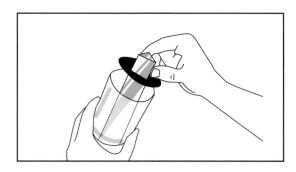

6 Hold the mirror system in the middle of one foam circle and trace around it. Repeat with the other foam circle. Carefully cut out each triangle to leave a triangular hole in the middle of each foam circle. Fit the circles over each end of the mirror system.

7 Slide the mirrors and foam circles into the bottle so one end of the mirrors fits into the bottle cap eyepiece.

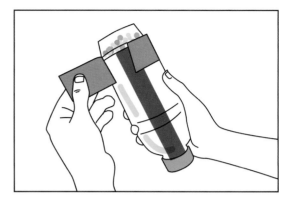

8 Fill the object chamber with goodies. Close the chamber and seal it.

9 Attach the chamber to the bottle with a strip of tape. Let your eyes drink in the beautiful visions!

VARIATION

Sharpen Your Focus

Adapt the same directions to a sturdy nondisposable bottle.

Personalize a See-Through Scope

Is your bottle clear? Decorate this tube from the inside out! Slip a piece of decorative paper, a drawing, or a photo inside the bottle. The size will depend on the bottle you have chosen. You can also wrap colorful duct tape around the end of the mirror system (the part you can see through the bottle) to brighten things up.

ASK A GROWN-UP!

Rocket Scope

If you hand this rocket to a friend and say, "Look at my kaleidoscope!" she might think you are from outer space. But one peek inside and she will soar into orbit! If you don't want to draw your own rocket fin attachment, look on page 115 for a template to trace.

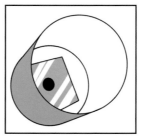

MATERIALS:

- Mailing tube with one end cap (2" diameter x 13")
- Drill bit with ¼" bit
- 1" square of clear, flat plastic
- 1 sheet of black paper, to fit the tube
- 3 strips of poster frame plastic (11" x 1⅜") (see page 69)
- 2 small rubber bands
- Tape
- 2¾" circle of clear, flat plastic
- Strip of foam with adhesive backing (½" x 9")
- Silver wrapping paper
- Space-themed stickers
- Assorted goodies
- Colored plastic Easter egg (the kind with two halves)
- Colored duct tape
- Pencil
- Printer paper
- Scissors
- 2 sheets of foam

❶ Ask an adult to drill a hole in the center of the mailing tube's end cap.

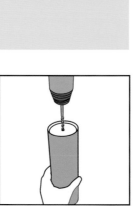

❷ Drop the plastic square into the tube so it covers the eyehole. Make sure it covers the inside of the eyehole—this piece protects your eye!

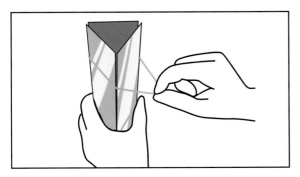

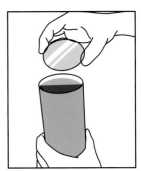

3 Arrange the strips of poster frame plastic in a 3-D equilateral triangle—oriented just like your master scope mirrors. Slip the rubber bands over the ends to hold the triangle in place. Tape around the outside of the triangle to hold it together. Remove the rubber bands.

4 Curl up the black paper and slip it inside the tube. Slide the three-mirror system into the tube. It should rest on the plastic eyeguard that you made in Step 2. Drop the circle of plastic into the tube, so that it rests on the mirror system.

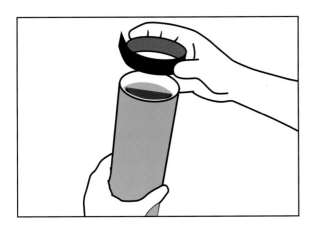

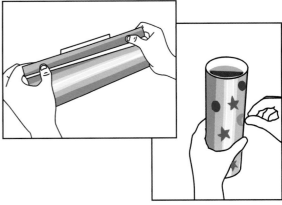

5 Peel the protective paper from the foam strip, and press the sticky side to the inside of the can, forming a collar that will hold the clear circle in place. The strip should be flush with the plastic circle—check to make sure that there are no gaps between the two. You have just created the object chamber of your kaleidoscope inside the tube.

6 Tape the wrapping paper around the tube. Decorate it with space-themed stickers— think stars, moons, planets, satellites . . . anything you want!

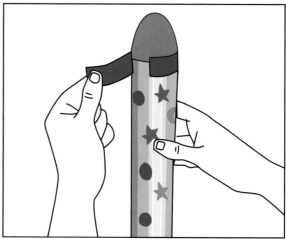

7 Fill the object chamber with goodies.

8 To seal them in, place the pointy half of an Easter egg on the end of the tube. Secure it with colored tape. This is the rocket's nose!

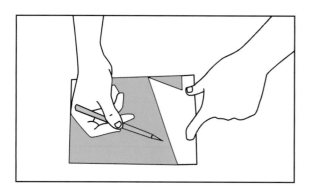

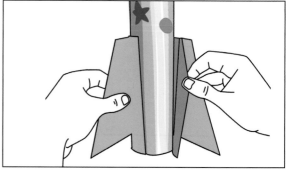

9 Draw a fin template (like the one in the picture above—or use the template on page 115) onto a piece of printer paper, with an extra ½" flap on the thickest side of the fin. Cut out the fin template and trace it at least six times on the sheet of foam. Cut out the shapes.

10 Glue two fins together—leaving the ½" flaps on each fin open. Open the flaps and glue them to the tube—so that the fin sticks out—at the end opposite the rocket's nose. Repeat for the remaining fins. Don't let the fins extend beyond the end of the tube, or your rocket won't stand up. (And we don't want those fins poking you in the eye.) Now get ready for a peek into outer space!

Dollar Store Extravaganza

Are you ready for a kaleidoscopic extravaganza? Almost all of the materials in this project can be purchased at a dollar or party store. If you don't have a rubber ball, make a chamber instead. Experiment with all kinds of round and cylindrical containers. It's amazing how many you will find once you start looking.

MATERIALS:

- Foam can holder
- Ruler
- Paper
- Thin permanent marker
- Scissors
- 2 circles of clear, flat plastic (2½" and 2" in diameter)
- Craft paper
- Clear tape
- Mailing tube with end caps (2½" x 10")
- Plastic spring toy, like a Slinky
- Colored duct tape
- 3 strips of poster frame plastic (1¾" x 9½") (see page 69)
- Sheet of black paper, the length of the tube
- Soft, transparent rubber bouncing ball, about 1½" to 3" diameter
- Assorted goodies
- Craft foam (optional)

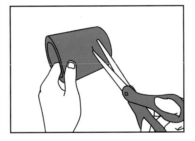

❶ Use paper as a straight edge to measure and mark a line 1½" from the bottom of the foam can holder with the thin permanent marker. Carefully cut along the line with scissors. This piece will become the eyepiece.

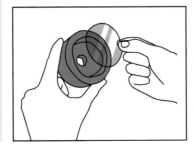

❷ Drop the 2½" plastic circle into the eyepiece. Make sure it covers the hole completely—this piece protects your eye!

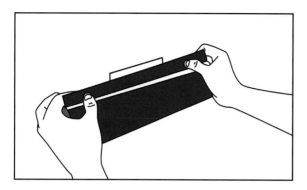

❸ Wrap craft paper around the mailing tube and tape it in place.

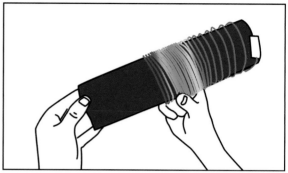

❹ Slide the spring toy over the tube. Attach the ends of the spring to the ends of the tube with small pieces of duct tape. Fold the tape over the inside of the tube to secure.

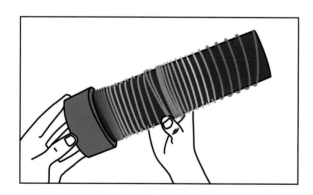

❺ Push the foam eyepiece onto one end of the tube.

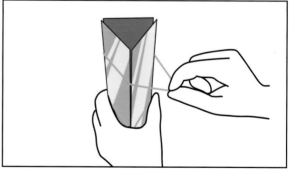

❻ Arrange the strips of poster frame plastic in a 3-D equilateral triangle—oriented just like your master scope mirrors. Slip the rubber bands over the ends to hold the triangle in place, then tape around the outside of the triangle to hold it together. Remove the rubber bands.

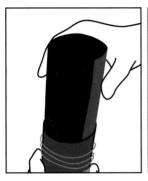
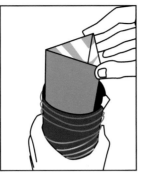
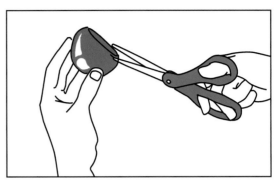

7 Curl up the black paper and slip it inside the tube. Slide the mirror system inside the tube. It should rest on the eyeguard that you inserted in Step 2. If necessary, stick some craft foam inside the tube to keep the mirror system from rattling around.

8 Ask an adult to cut a 2" hole in the rubber ball with scissors.

9 Fill the ball halfway with goodies.

10 Cover the open end of the ball with the 2" plastic circle. Wrap a strip of duct tape around the ball so that half of the tape is stuck to the ball and half is just sticking up over the edge. Snip flaps in the tape about ½" apart, and fold the flaps over to seal the object chamber.

11 Put the object chamber into the tube so that the clear circle faces the mirrors. Wrap another strip of duct tape around the top of the tube and the ball to keep everything in place. Now take a look!

Magic Wand Scope

The next time you get a new tube of toothpaste, save the box. You can make a two-mirror kaleidoscope while you shine up those pearly whites. We are going to transform a boring activity into a tube of fireworks.

You'll also need a narrow tube to make into a liquid wand. But before using the tube, make sure it will not leak. Put some water in the tube, seal it up, and stand it on the cap end overnight in a cup. If there is a little puddle in the cup in the morning, your wand is too leaky—pick another tube to test.

MATERIALS:

- Large toothpaste box
- Scissors
- Hole punch
- 1¼" square of clear, flat plastic
- Clear tape
- Pencil
- Clear, narrow bead tube with cap
- Cuticle scissors
- 2 strips of poster frame plastic (2" x 7") (see page 69)
- Strip of black matte board (1½" x 7")
- 2 small rubber bands
- Assorted goodies
- Water
- Colored duct tape

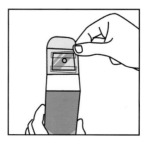

❶ Cut off the two smaller flaps of the toothpaste box. Use the hole punch to make a hole in the center of the remaining end flap.

❷ Tape the plastic square to the inside of the flap, over the hole you made in Step 1.

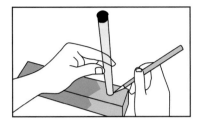

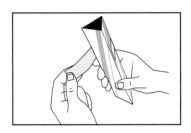

3 Turn the box around to work with the other end. Trace the diameter of the small tube on opposite sides of the box, as shown. Cut out the circles with cuticle scissors. The tube should fit through both holes, but remain snug.

4 Arrange the strips of poster frame plastic and the strip of black matte board in a 3-D triangle. Slip rubber bands over both ends to hold the triangle in place, then tape around the outside of the triangle to hold it together. Remove the rubber bands.

5 Slide the mirror system into the box. Tape the end of the mirror system to the box to keep it from sliding into the tube. Fold the eye-hole flap back into place and tape it down.

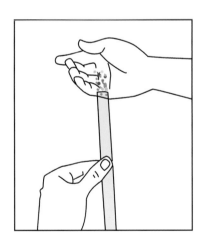

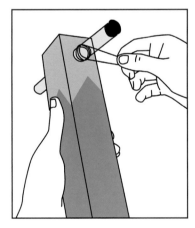

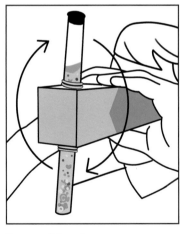

6 Remove the small tube from the box and fill it half-way with goodies. Then add water to fill, and secure the cap. Wrap a small piece of colored duct tape around the cap to prevent leakage.

7 Slide the tube back through the holes. Wrap a small rubber band around either side of the tube, close to the holes, to keep the tube from falling out.

8 Hold the scope, as shown, to your eye, so that the chamber is vertical. Flip it the other way and watch the fireworks!

All Bottled Up

You can become a genius inventor in

this project. There is no limit to what your imagination can come up with. If you want to experiment with different containers, do it! You can try all kinds of caps on all kinds of tubes. You will be amazed that you can find so many pieces that are like ready-made kaleidoscope parts. To some people, these kaleidoscope materials might be trash. But to a kaleidoscope artist like you, it's treasure!

MATERIALS:

- Empty plastic bottle
- Hacksaw
- Sandpaper
- Ruler
- Paper
- Thin permanent marker
- Scissors
- Clear, flat plastic
- 3 strips of poster frame plastic (¼" shorter than the bottle) (see page 69)
- 2 rubber bands
- Tape
- Sheet of black paper, to fit the bottle
- 2 empty, clear water bottles, dried completely
- Assorted goodies
- Colored duct tape

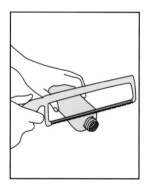

❶ Ask an adult to saw off the spout of the first bottle as close to the top of the bottle as possible. The remaining hole will be a perfect eyehole. Smooth down the edges with a piece of sandpaper. Note: If this end of the bottle is not flat, it may not sit well on the table.

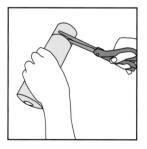

❷ Use paper as a straight edge to measure and mark a line around the outside of the bottle about 1" from the bottom with thin permanent marker. Cut off the bottom piece with scissors.

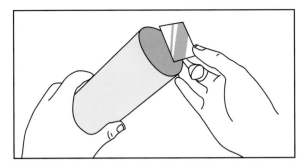

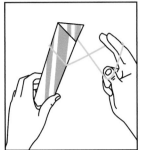

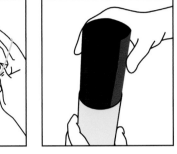

3 Cut the clear plastic into a square big enough to cover the eyehole. Drop it into the tube. Make sure the plastic circle covers the hole completely—this piece protects your eye!

4 Arrange the strips of poster frame plastic in a 3-D equilateral triangle—oriented just like your master scope mirrors. Slip the rubber bands over the ends to hold the triangle in place. Tape around the outside of the triangle to hold it together. Remove the rubber bands.

5 Curl up the black paper and slip it inside the tube. Slide the three-mirror system into the tube. It should rest on the eyeguard that you inserted in Step 3.

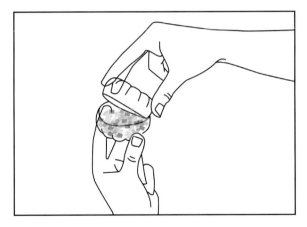

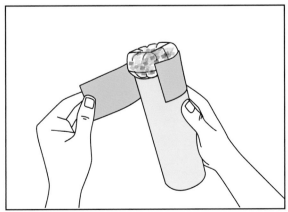

6 To make the object chamber, measure and mark a line 1" from the bottom of each of the clear water bottles, using paper as a staight edge. Cut off the bottom pieces with scissors. Fill one of these bottoms with goodies. Fit the other bottom on top, tucking the edges into the first one. Tape them together around the seam with colored duct tape.

7 Tape the chamber to the open end of the bottle. Look through the other end!

ASK A GROWN-UP!

Oh Honey!

After you fill your belly with honey,

what can you do with that empty honey bear? Fill his belly with a kaleidoscope! This is a scope that would look great with some decoration, so go wild! Give your bear a cute shirt or a sparkly necklace of glitter. When you're decorating the wheels (your bear's feet!), feel free to experiment with other kinds of see-through labels or stickers—anything that lets light in.

MATERIALS

- Cap from a sports drink bottle
- Drill with ¼" bit
- 1" square of clear, flat plastic
- Clear tape
- 3 strips of poster frame plastic (1" x 6") (see page 69)
- 24-ounce honey bear squeeze bottle, cleaned and dried completely
- Sheet of black paper to fit around the triangle
- 2 circles of clear, flat plastic (2¾" in diameter)
- See-through stickers
- 2 flat thumbtacks
- Colored duct tape
- Stickers

❶ Ask an adult to drill a hole in the bottle cap to make the eyepiece. Tape the plastic square to the inside of the cap.

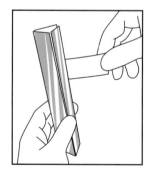

❷ Arrange the strips of poster frame plastic in a 3-D equilateral triangle—oriented just like your master scope mirrors. Slip the rubber bands over the ends to hold the triangle in place. Tape around the outside of the triangle to hold it together. Remove the rubber bands.

❸ Fit the black paper around the triangle and slip them inside the squeeze bottle. They should fit snugly.

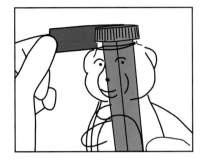 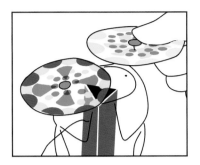 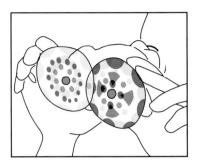

4 Fit the eyepiece onto the open end of the bottle and use colored duct tape to secure it.

5 Decorate the plastic circles with see-through stickers. Punch a hole in the middle of the circles with the thumbtack, and then push them through the bottom of the bottle on both sides.

6 Use stickers to decorate the outside of the bottle. Give your bear's new "feet" a spin as you look inside . . . how sweet it is!

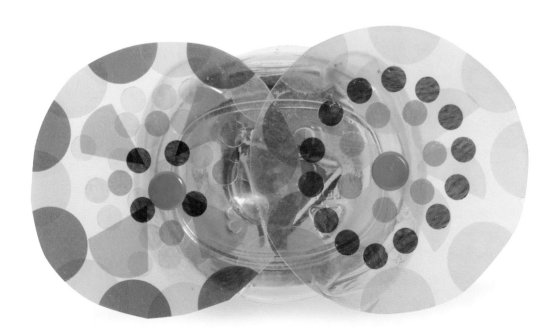

ASK A GROWN-UP!

Beam Me Up

This kaleidoscope might not help you see in the dark, but with a few simple changes, a colorful plastic flashlight can brighten your day in a new way. If you don't have a plastic flashlight at home, go to the dollar store to get the makings of this sturdy scope. And it comes with the object chamber built right in! The clear plastic lens of the flashlight becomes the outer disk of your object chamber. It's a great scope for trying out different combinations of objects because the end screws on and off.

MATERIALS:

- Plastic flashlight
- Drill with a ¼" bit
- 2 circles of clear, flat plastic (¾" in diameter)
- 3 strips of poster frame plastic (about 1¼" x 6¼") (see page 69)
- 2 rubber bands
- Tape
- Glue
- Assorted goodies

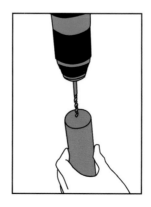

❶ Unscrew the lightbulb end of the flashlight. Take out the bulb assembly and the spring that holds the batteries in place (it's usually a silver funnel shape)—you won't need them for this project.

❷ Ask an adult to drill a hole in the center of the other end of the flashlight (the handle). Drop one of the plastic circles into the flashlight tube over the hole. Make sure it covers the hole completely—this piece protects your eye!

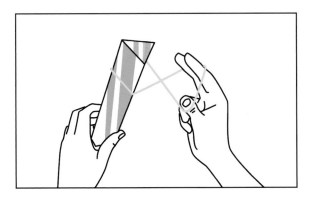

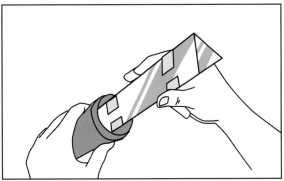

❸ Arrange the strips of poster frame plastic in a 3-D equilateral triangle—oriented just like your master scope mirrors. Slip the rubber bands over the ends to hold the triangle in place. Tape around the outside of the triangle to hold it together. Remove the rubber bands.

❹ Slide the three-mirror system into the tube. It should rest on the eyeguard that you inserted in Step 2.

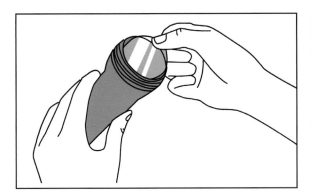

❺ Fit the other plastic circle into the tube on top of the mirrors. Dot a few blobs of glue around the edges of the circle to hold it in place. Let dry.

❻ Fill this chamber with goodies. Screw the end cap back on. Now check out the view!

ASK A GROWN-UP!

Sideways Scope

Have you ever bought juice or milk in bulk? Sometimes the big bottles come with a handle that holds two together. I bet you threw away that plastic holder. Next time, save it, because you can use it to create this Sideways Scope. It's a *lateral* turner, and it's called that because you rotate it a bit differently than you would your master scope. If your container can hold liquid without leaking, try a liquid chamber (see Ocean Slow-Motion Scope, page 58). Just don't forget to decorate it!

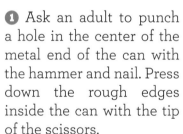

MATERIALS:

- 3" x 9" potato chip can (5¾ ounces) and lid, cleaned and dried completely
- Hammer
- Nail
- Scissors
- 2" square of clear, flat plastic
- 3 strips of poster frame plastic (8¼" x 2⅜") (see page 69)
- 2 rubber bands
- Clear tape
- Sheet of black paper, the length of the tube
- 2 plastic handles that would hold four juice bottles
- Strong kitchen shears
- Rubber bands
- Colored duct tape
- Spice jar that will fit into the round opening of the handles
- Assorted goodies

① Ask an adult to punch a hole in the center of the metal end of the can with the hammer and nail. Press down the rough edges inside the can with the tip of the scissors.

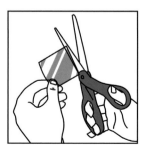

② Drop the square of plastic into the can so it covers the eyehole. Make sure it covers the hole completely—this piece protects your eye!

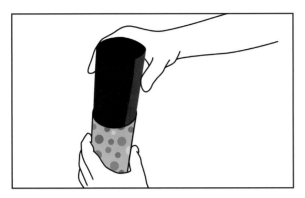

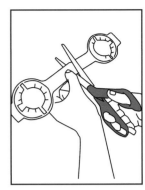

❸ Curl up the black paper and slide it inside the tube. Arrange the strips of poster frame plastic in a 3-D equilateral triangle—oriented just like your master scope mirrors. Slip the rubber bands over the ends to hold the triangle in place. Tape around the outside of the triangle to hold it together. Remove the rubber bands.

❹ Slide the three-mirror system into the tube. It should rest on the eyeguard that you inserted in Step 2.

❺ Ask an adult to cut one circle off each handle with strong kitchen shears, as shown.

❻ Hold these two pieces on opposite sides of the tube, and wrap a rubber band around them. Wrap duct tape over the rubber band to secure the plastic pieces.

❼ Fill the spice jar chamber with goodies, and then push through the holes in the plastic handle. Rotate the jar to view!

For Good Measure

This kaleidoscope is the quickest, straightest scope in the West (or the North, East, and South). It's a simple teleidoscope. If you select colored rulers, you will see flashes of those colors in the view. If you want to continue to use the rulers for their original purpose (measuring and drawing a straight line against the edge), just use a bit of clear tape to hold them together—you can have a multifunctional teleidoscope.

MATERIALS:
- 3 new polished and shiny plastic rulers
- 3 rubber bands

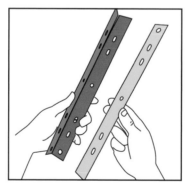

1 Arrange the rulers, with the flattest side facing in, to form a 3-D equilateral triangle—oriented just like your master scope mirrors.

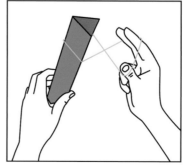

2 Slip the rubber bands over the rulers to hold them together. That's it! No more steps, except to look through one end at the world around you.

VARIATION

MATERIALS:

- 2½" square of thin cardboard
- Sparkly stickers
- Decorative tape
- Pencil with eraser
- Pushpin

Sparkly Wheel Scope

Although the kaleidoscope project at left is impressively quick, you may want to spend a bit more time on it to get a lot more to look at. To add a little more bling to this kaleidoscope, you can attach a wheel to the end.

But guess what? Your kaleidoscope "wheel" does not have to be round! A square rotating on an axis can do the same job—provided that it is bigger than the shaft of the mirror system.

❶ Decorate the square of cardboard with an array of sparkly stickers and colorful tape. If you decorate both sides, you can turn it over, so you'll have twice as much to look at!

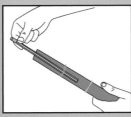

❷ Slide the pencil under the rubber bands. Let the eraser hang over one end of the kaleidoscope.

❸ Attach the square "wheel" to the eraser with the pushpin. Give it a spin and take a look!

Great Big Wonderful Wheel

Step back and watch the world go 'round in circles! You can substitute any wheel from one of the many variations described on page 125 for the one in this kaleidoscope.

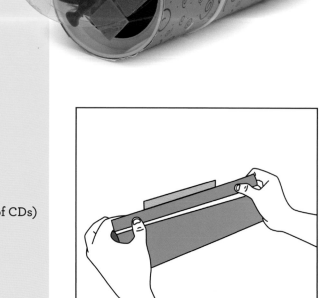

MATERIALS:

- 1 sheet of craft paper (12" x 12")
- Clear tape
- Mailing tube with end caps (3" in diameter, 12" long)
- Dime
- Pencil or pen
- 3 caps from ½ gallon milk cartons
- Drafting compass
- Small cuticle scissors
- 2 circles of clear, flat plastic (2¾" in diameter)
- Black construction paper (12" x 12")
- 3 strips of poster frame plastic (each 2.5" x 11") (see page 69)
- 2 rubber bands
- Clear CD (from the top of a new stack of CDs)
- Blank or used CD
- Decorations for the CDs
- ½" dowel (½" in diameter, 12" long)
- 3 zip ties (at least 8" long)
- Clothespin (the kind with a spring)

❶ Wrap the craft paper around the mailing tube and tape it in place.

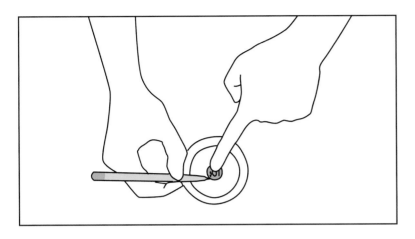

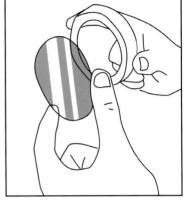

❷ Place the dime on one of the mailing tube end caps and trace around it. Use the drafting compass to draw a circle 2¼" in diameter on the other cap. Cut out the shapes with the small scissors. The cap with the dime-size hole will be the eyepiece, and the cap with the larger hole will go on the chamber end.

❸ Tape the clear plastic circles inside the two caps. Make sure they cover the holes completely—these pieces protect your eye!

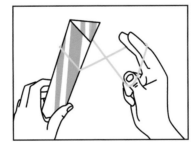

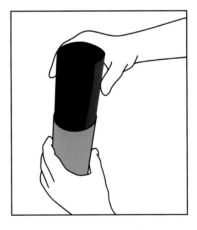

❹ Place the cap with the biggest hole onto the tube. Secure it with tape.

❺ Arrange the poster frame plastic in a 3-D equilateral triangle—oriented just like your master scope mirrors. Slip the rubber bands over the ends to hold the triangle in place and tape around the outside to secure. Remove the rubber bands.

❻ Curl up the black paper and slip it inside the tube. Slide the three-mirror system into the tube. Put the eyepiece on the open end of the tube. Secure it with tape.

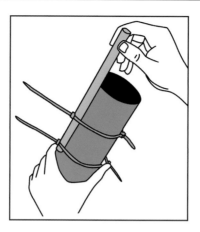

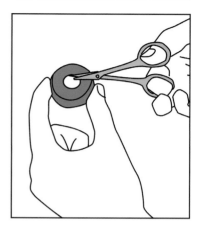

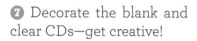

7 Decorate the blank and clear CDs—get creative!

8 Attach the dowel to the outside of the tube with zip ties, lengthwise, so that 2½" hang over the end of the tube, opposite the eyepiece.

9 Place the dime in the middle of one of the milk carton caps and trace around it. Carefully cut out the circle with small scissors. Repeat with the two remaining caps.

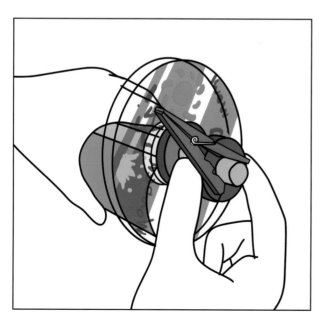

10 Slip one of the milk caps over the dowel. Then slip on the decorated blank CD, and then another cap. Repeat with the second decorated CD and the last milk cap. Keep the stack in place with the clothespin.

The Double Take

When you want to share something beautiful and can't quite describe it, it can be frustrating. When you look through a kaleidoscope and see the *best design ever,* you want to share it. But by the time you pass the scope to a friend, the pieces will have shifted and the design will be different. Here's a scope that will let you and a friend look at the same kaleidoscope together.

MATERIALS:

- 2 potato chip cans (3" x 9") and lids, cleaned and dried completely
- Hammer
- Nail
- Scissors
- Two 2" squares of clear, flat plastic
- 6 strips of poster frame plastic (8¼" x 2⅜") (see page 69)
- 2 sheets of black paper, the same length as the can
- 4 rubber bands
- Masking tape
- Assorted goodies
- Clear object chamber to fit in between the tubes (bead storage containers work well)

❶ Ask an adult to punch a hole in the center of the metal end of each can with the hammer and nail. Press down the rough edges inside the can with the tip of the scissors.

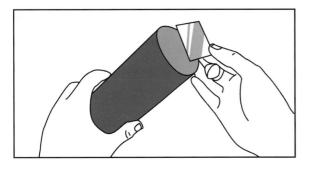

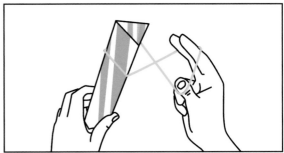

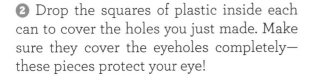

2 Drop the squares of plastic inside each can to cover the holes you just made. Make sure they cover the eyeholes completely—these pieces protect your eye!

3 Arrange three strips of poster frame plastic in a 3-D equilateral triangle—oriented just like your master scope mirrors. Slip the rubber bands over the ends to hold the triangle in place. Tape around the outside of the triangle to hold it together. Remove the rubber bands.

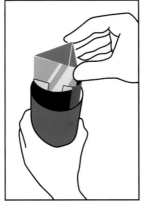

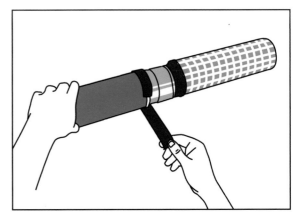

4 Repeat Step 3 to make another mirror system. Curl up the sheets of black paper and slip one into each tube. Then slide the mirror systems into the tubes. They should rest on the eyeguards you inserted in Step 2.

5 Fit your goodies into the object chamber and close it up. Use masking tape to secure the object chamber between the viewing ends of the tubes. Now you and your friend can look at the same vision together.

Camera Capture

Almost everyone has a small camera nowadays—most people use the one on their phone! With this project, you can make a special kaleidoscope that acts a little like a distorted photo booth. Rig it to your phone or camera to take crazy pictures of your friends (or whatever you want—flowers, landscapes, your dog . . . the list is endless). To start, you'll need something that almost anyone can find right in his or her refrigerator—a plastic milk or juice container. (Try to find one with a screw cap.) With a bit of recycling savvy, you can make something that will bring you memories for a lifetime.

Now you can take pictures to capture your unique designs forever. The closer you are to the subject, the better the image will be. Experiment with colors and shapes. If your camera has video capabilities, give that a spin. Add a little music and you could have a YouTube–worthy show.

MATERIALS:

- Ruler
- Thin permanent marker
- 1-quart plastic milk container, cleaned and dried completely
- Scissors
- 3 strips of mirror paper with adhesive backing (2¾" x 7½" x 1⅛")
- 3 strips of poster frame plastic (2¾" x 7½" x 1⅛") (see pages 69 and 116 for techniques and templates)
- 2 rubber bands
- Black craft tape
- Double-sided mounting tape
- 1 piece of colored craft foam (4" x 9")
- Camera or smartphone

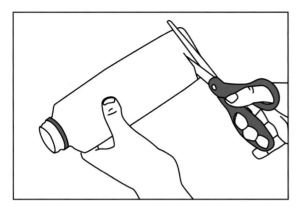

❶ Use a piece of paper as a straight edge to draw a line to measure and mark 1" from the bottom of the milk container around all four sides. Carefully cut along the lines with scissors and discard the bottom of the container.

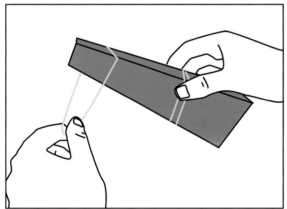

❷ Remove the protective backing from the mirror paper. Press one strip to each strip of plastic. Arrange the strips in a 3-D tapered triangular tube—oriented just like your master scope mirrors. Wrap the rubber bands around the ends to hold the tube in place.

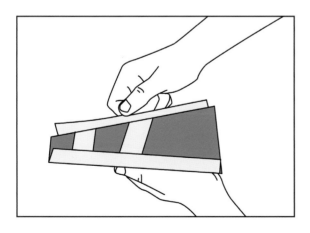

❸ Make sure the edges are lined up neatly and wrap tape in a spiral around each end of the triangle to secure it. Seal the long edges with black tape so that no light can leak into the mirror system. Remove the rubber bands.

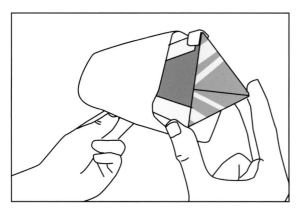

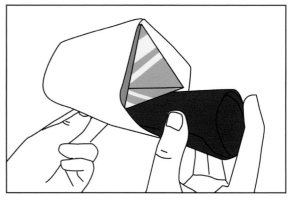

④ Place a 1" piece of double-sided mounting tape on one point of the wide end of the triangle. Carefully slide the triangle into the milk container so the narrow end of the mirror fits up against the small round opening. One side of the triangle should sit flat on the little ledge inside the container. The tape will keep it in place.

⑤ Roll up the piece of craft foam and slide it into the big space in the container, to keep the mirrors from rattling.

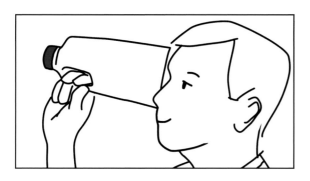

⑥ Now you can hold the handle of the milk container and point the small end of your camera scope over colorful things. Take your camera and point it right into the wide end of the triangle. You will see patterns fly by on the viewfinder as you move this teleidoscope around. Now you're ready to take a picture!

VARIATION

If you want a really snappy piece of camera equipment that will make even greater photos, use a 1¼" clear acrylic ball. Use small scissors to cut a 1"-diameter hole in the cap of the container. The 1¼" ball should fit right into the little spout of the container. Screw the cap over the ball to secure it.

A Chorus Line

Have you ever seen a show with a line of people singing and dancing? That line of people is called a *chorus line*. The reflection is made when mirrors face each other like in The Hall of Mirrors project (page 21). As you look at the chorus line of images through your scope, you may feel the need to burst out in a little song and dance. Ta-da!

MATERIALS:

- 1 sheet of black craft foam with adhesive backing (8" x 12")
- 2 strips of poster frame plastic (2" x 8") (see page 69)
- 2 strips of black matte board (¾" x 8")
- Scissors
- 2 rubber bands
- Unsharpened pencil with an eraser
- Two 8" zip ties
- Clear tape
- 1" square of lightweight cardboard
- 1 CD, blank or used
- Glue
- Colored drinking straws, sequins, and any other wheel decorations
- 1 large pushpin

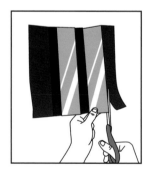

❶ Place the sheet of foam on a flat work surface, adhesive side up, and peel off the protective paper. Lay a strip of plastic onto the sticky surface of the foam. Place a strip of black paper next to it, with a little space in between—no more than ⅛". Repeat with the remaining plastic strip, and then the last black paper strip.

❷ Cut around all four strips with scissors and trim off any extra foam. Carefully fold the mirror system into a rectangle.

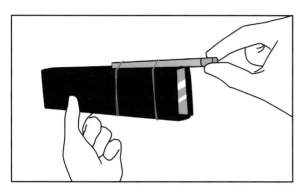 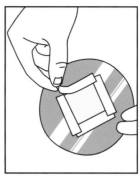 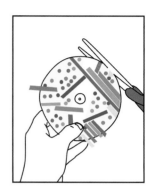

3 Wrap two rubber bands around the rectangle. Slide the pencil under the rubber bands so that the eraser end hangs over the end of the mirror system. Secure the pencil with the two zip ties and remove the rubber bands. Trim the zip ties with scissors.

4 Tape the square of cardboard over the hole in the CD. Cut up pieces of colored drinking straws—varying in size—and glue them onto the disk in any direction you want. Glue sequins into any spots that are not covered.

5 Position the decorated side of the disk so that it faces into the mirror system, and then use the pushpin to attach the wheel to the pencil eraser, through the center of the cardboard square. Spin the disk and watch the chorus line dance before your eyes!

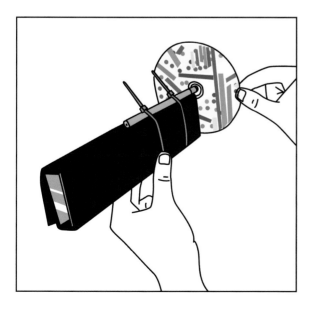

ASK A GROWN-UP!

Isn't It Marbleous?

A two-piece toothbrush holder will make this scope a bit crazy—you might think you've lost your marbles! If you take it apart to put in a different marble, open it gently so your marble doesn't go flying across the room!

MATERIALS:

- Small cuticle scissors
- Two-part cylindrical travel toothbrush holder that fits together at the center
- Piece of clear, flat plastic
- 2 strips of poster frame plastic (¾" wide, ½" shorter than the holder) (see page 69)
- Strip of black matte board (½" wide, ½" shorter than the holder)
- Sheet of black paper, the size of the holder
- 2 rubber bands
- Tape
- Translucent marble no larger than the inner diameter of your tube

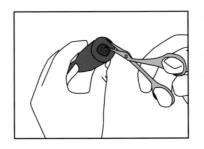

❶ Ask an adult to cut a ½" hole in the center of each end of the toothbrush holder with the cuticle scissors.

❷ Cut a circle of clear plastic larger than the hole but small enough to fit in the tube of the toothbrush holder. Drop it into one of the tubes to cover the hole—this end will be the eyehole.

 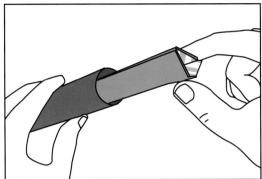

❸ Arrange the strips of poster frame plastic and black matte board in a 3-D equilateral triangle—oriented just like your master scope mirrors. Slip the rubber bands over the ends to hold the triangle in place. Tape around the outside of the triangle to hold it together. Remove the rubber bands. Curl up the black paper and slip it into the half of the holder with the eyehole. Slide the mirror system into the same half.

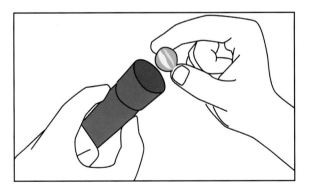 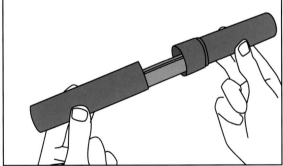

❹ Plop a marble into the other half of the holder and carefully fit the two holder halves together. Don't push too much, or you might distort the mirrors. The marble should remain pushed up against the hole but should be able to roll freely—you can adjust how tight it is by pushing and pulling the two halves slightly. Now take a look!

Crystal Vision Teleidoscope

Remember the teleidoscope you made back on page 42? That was a simpler version of this cool variation. To make the *best* kind of teleidoscope, you need a lens that reduces the image. A clear ball of glass or plastic will bring the world beyond all the way to the edge of your mirrors. With this lens, the image will be reflected into perfect symmetry all the time. Although a clear ball may not be the easiest thing to find, it *is* worth the search. Novelty magnets, drawer pulls, a ball from a chandelier, a large marble, or a big bead from a necklace will all work as long as you find a tube to fit it.

MATERIALS:
- Pencil
- Printer paper
- Tube with a diameter close to the size of the ball
- Scissors
- Ruler
- White craft glue
- Clear or translucent ball
- Sheet of poster frame plastic
- 2 rubber bands
- Clear tape
- Sheet of black paper, the same length as the tube
- Circle of clear, flat plastic the same diameter as the tube
- Colored duct tape

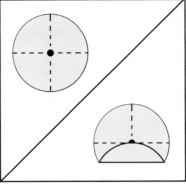

1 Trace a circle around the tube on a piece of paper. Draw a second circle ⅛" inside the first to account for the width of the tube. Cut out that circle. Fold the circle in half twice to make a point where the two fold lines intersect. That is the center of your circle. Fold up the bottom half of the circle to meet the fold line at the circle's equator, as shown. Unfold it, and measure the length of the new fold to determine the width of your mirrors. The length of your mirrors should be 1" shorter than the tube (at minimum, 2½ times the mirror's width).

2 Dab a bit of glue inside one end of the tube and insert the ball. Let dry. The glue will hold the ball in place.

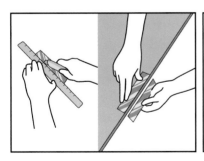
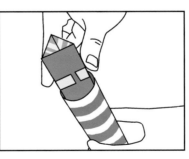
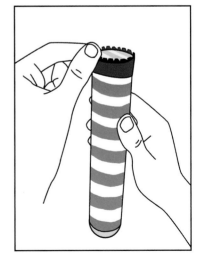

3 Ask an adult to cut the poster frame plastic into three rectangles, using the score and snap method on page 69 and the dimensions you calculated in Step 1. Arrange the strips of poster frame plastic in a 3-D equilateral triangle—oriented just like your master scope mirrors. Slip the rubber bands over the ends to hold the triangle in place. Tape around the outside of the triangle to hold it together. Remove the rubber bands. Curl up the black paper and slip it into the tube. Slide the three-mirror system into the tube.

4 Place the plastic circle on the open end and seal it with colored duct tape.

Facet-nating Scope

In this project, you will scan the environment to see dazzling sights. Adapt a basic kaleidoscope by using a clear, multifaceted crystal knob: the kind people hang in the window to make rainbows. Multifaceted crystal balls can be easy to find, if you know where to look—you can find them in the form of a light fixture pull or a lamp finial (ornament). Party stores also sell multiplying viewers that usually come six to a package. They have multifaceted "lenses" that pop out pretty easily.

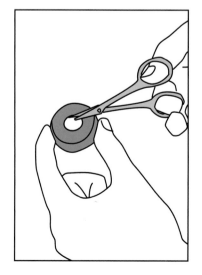

MATERIALS:

- Scissors
- Decorative paper
- Small cardboard tube
- Tape
- Plastic milk bottle cap
- Small cuticle scissors
- Clear, flat plastic
- Colored duct tape
- Ruler
- Thin permanent marker
- 3 strips of poster frame plastic (1" shorter than the tube) (see page 69)
- Sheet of black paper, the same length as the tube
- 2 rubber bands
- Faceted crystal drawer knob, with its screw, that will fit inside the tube

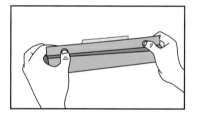

❶ Use scissors to cut a piece of decorative paper to fit the tube. Cover the tube with the paper and secure it with tape.

❷ Cut a hole ½" in diameter in the center of the milk bottle cap with the small scissors. Cut a circle out of the clear plastic that's small enough to fit into the milk bottle cap. Place it in the cap to complete the eyepiece. Make sure the plastic covers the eyehole completely— this piece protects your eye! Attach the eyepiece to one end of the tube with duct tape.

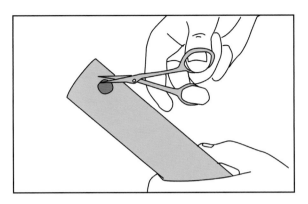

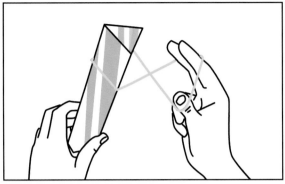

3 Measure and mark a dot ½" from the open end of the tube. Cut one small hole, ½" in diameter, over the dot.

4 Arrange the strips of poster frame plastic in a 3-D equilateral triangle—oriented just like your master scope mirrors. Slip the rubber bands over the ends to hold the triangle in place. Tape around the outside of the triangle to hold it together. Remove the rubber bands. Curl up the black paper and slip it into the tube. Slide the mirror system into the tube. It should rest on the eyeguard that you inserted in Step 2.

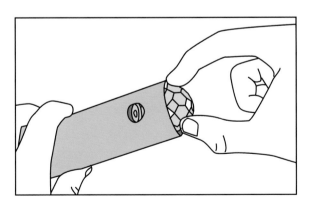

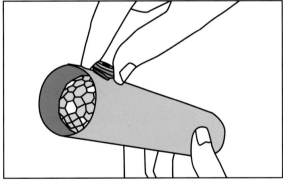

5 Fit the drawer knob into the open end of the tube.

6 Wrap a rubber band around the head of the screw to keep it from falling back through the hole. Turn the crystal as you look through the eyepiece. It's *facet*-nating, isn't it?

Showing Off Your Scope

Display Stands

You have made some really cool kaleidoscopes . . . so don't hide them in a box! Keep them out to share with others. A display stand can show off your beautiful creation and help position the scope at the best angle for viewing—just like an old-fashioned parlor scope. Your stand doesn't have to be old-fashioned, though.

When you're selecting a stand, match up the scope you want to display with the size of the opening. You might be able to find something like a doll stand, candleholder, pencil cup, or cup holder to serve as a quick-and-easy kaleidoscope stand. Use the stand just as it is, or decorate it to match your scope. *Always be sure the stand is strong enough to hold your scope.*

HERE ARE SOME IDEAS IN CASE YOU WANT TO MAKE YOUR OWN:

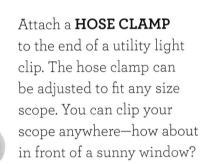

Cover a **SMALL BOX** with wrapping paper. Tape two foam doorknob hangers to either side.

Attach a **HOSE CLAMP** to the end of a utility light clip. The hose clamp can be adjusted to fit any size scope. You can clip your scope anywhere—how about in front of a sunny window?

Take an empty **TUBE** from a roll of packing tape and cut it in half lengthwise. Paint, or cover the halves with foam or fabric. Glue the halves together, or glue each half to the top of a shoe box.

Glue a stack of plastic **BANGLE BRACELETS** or napkin rings to a base of sturdy cardboard or a plastic plate. Use craft foam inside to perfect the fit.

Light Up Your Scope!

Having trouble seeing in the dark?

Hardware stores have all sorts of little flashlights that can be adapted to light up your scope. LEDs (light-emitting diodes) make very small flashlights possible. Find one with a flexible neck (like a book light) and attach it to the end of your kaleidoscope tube so you can maneuver the light source. Just use a piece of colored duct tape to keep it in place—and be sure not to cover the on/off button!

Be sure you keep the *frosted* end cap in place. Some lighting can be very powerful and should not shine directly into your eyes without some type of filter.

Templates

Use tracing paper to transfer these shapes onto cardstock. If you have a copier, you can copy this page onto cardstock, cut out the shapes, and keep a set of templates in your artist's studio to trace around.

CIRCLE TEMPLATES

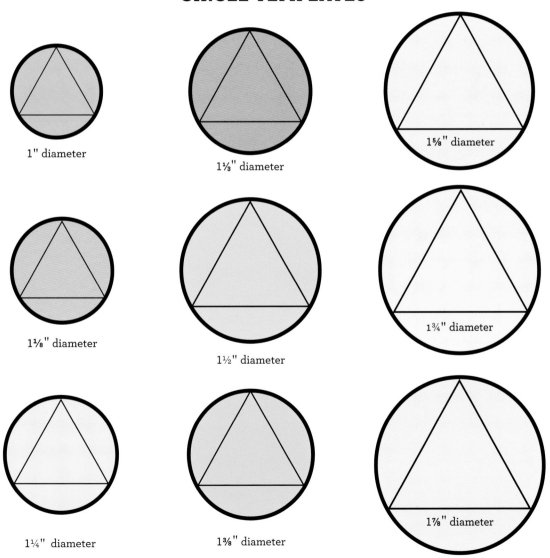

1" diameter

1⅓" diameter

1⅝" diameter

1⅛" diameter

1½" diameter

1¾" diameter

1¼" diameter

1⅜" diameter

1⅞" diameter

THE MIRROR MASK
TEMPLATES

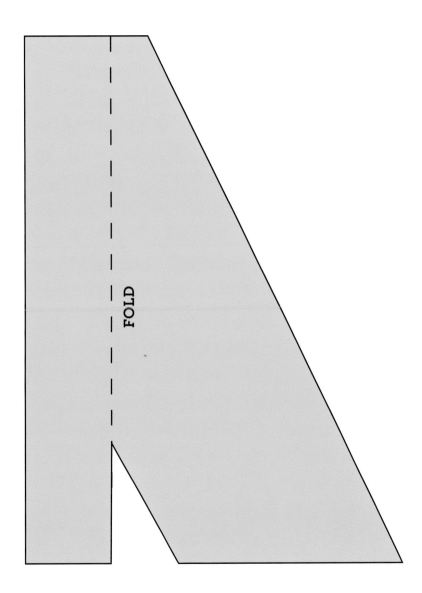

FOLD

ROCKET SCOPE
(Fin Template)

CAMERA CAPTURE
(Mirror Template)

TECHNIQUES FOR BUILDING YOUR OWN KALEIDOSCOPES

As you master the art of scope-making, there are certain things that have to be repeated from scope to scope. Here are some helpful hints that you'll want to refer to when you're making your own creations.

Make a Hole in the Center of a Container with an Attached Bottom

In many cases, you'll be recycling a tube for your kaleidoscope body that has an opening on just one end. You'll have to know how to create an eyehole to see through.

Metal cans: Ask an adult to punch a hole into the center of the can with a hammer and nail. Then push a pair of closed scissors into the nail hole and turn them around until you have widened the hole to about ½" across. When the hole is big enough, press down any rough edges inside the can with the tip of the scissors.

Punch hole using nail and hammer.

Widen hole with scissors.

Plastic containers: Place a dime (which is just the right size for an eyehole) on the center of the closed end and trace around it. Carefully cut out the hole with very small scissors (like cuticle scissors).

Of course, if you have an adult around, there's a much easier way of making a hole in the center of the container. Ask him or her to drill a hole for you! Drills come with many different sizes of bits, so you'll have endless possibilities for eyehole size.

Cut out a hole with small (cuticle) scissors.

Make an End Cap for Any Size Tube

Trace a circle onto a piece of recycled plastic that is the same size as the diameter of the tube end. Cut out the circle and place it on top of the tube end. Wrap duct tape around the top edge of the tube so it sticks up above the rim. Snip the tape evenly all around. One at a time, fold the tabs over onto the disk (the tabs will overlap).

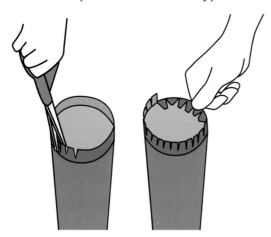

Snip the tape and fold the tabs over.

Clear Up a Fuzzy View with a Lens

The vision in your scope might look clear and sharp to you, but an older person might need reading glasses to see it. Those reading glasses can help clear up an image from the inside of your scope. Pop a lens out of a pair of plastic reading glasses and drop it into your scope at the eyehole end—before you insert the mirrors—to see what it does to the image.

A lens from reading glasses can sharpen the image in a scope.

Bisect a Circle

You'll need to know how to bisect a circle so that you can determine how wide to cut your mirrors. First, follow the steps for finding the center of a circle: Trace the outline (the circumference) of the tube you want to use onto a piece of paper. Draw another circle ⅛" inside the outline to account for the width of the tube. Cut out that circle. Fold the circle in half, and then in half again. The point where the two fold lines intersect is the center of your circle.

Now, bisect the circle: Fold the bottom half of the circle up to meet the fold line at the circle's equator, as shown. Unfold it, and draw over the new fold line. Measure the length of the fold. That's how wide your mirrors should be.

How to Make a Three-Mirror System

In a three-mirror scope, the longer and thinner your mirrors are, the more reflections you will have. What if you wanted to use a very short, fat tube? It might not be long enough to reflect an entire pattern.

The width of your mirrors will be determined by the measurement you made in "Bisect a Circle," above. The length will be determined by the length of the tube and the width of the mirrors.

Here is the rule: The length of the mirror should be at least two and a half times its width. If you need mirrors 2" wide, you need to make sure they are at least 5" long. The mirrors can be longer if your tube is longer, but not shorter.

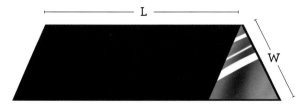

Width × 2½" = Length

How to Make a Two-Mirror System

In a scope with a two-mirror system, you will see a centered figure that may remind you of a pie cut into slices. The *vertex* of the system is the point where the mirrors come together. The closer you can get your eye to the vertex of a two-mirror system, the more symmetrical the image will be.

It's easy to transform your master scope into a two-mirror scope. Simply flip one mirror around so the nonreflective side is facing in. But, you can also trace the mirror onto a piece of thin, dark cardboard, cut out the rectangle, and slide that into the scope in place of the mirror.

To create a more complex pattern with a two-mirror system, change the angle between the two mirrors. The smaller the angle, the more slices you will see—and the more times the image will be reflected back and forth. Keep in mind that each time the image is reflected, it bends the light more and more, making the image darker and darker. So a very long, thin scope might not be as bright as one the same length with a larger diameter.

To create a narrow-angle system for two mirrors, trace the outline of the tube you want to use on a piece of tracing paper. Fold the circle in half to find its center. Use a compass to draw another circle, so that it is

Trace the outline of the tube.

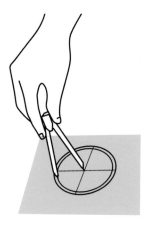

Draw a circle ⅛" inside the first circle.

⅛" inside the first circle (to compensate for the thickness of the tube walls).

Place the tracing paper over one of the angles on the Angle and Reflection Guide that follows so that the point of the angle touches the inside edge of the inner circle and the center line lies on top of the dotted line. If necessary, use a ruler to extend the angle lines until they touch the far side of the inner circle. Measure one of the lines to determine the width of the mirrors.

Now, draw a line connecting the two lines. That third line will be the width of the cardboard strip. The length will be the same as the other two mirrors.

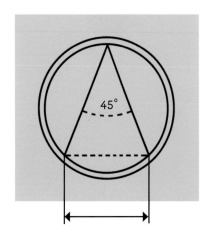

Determine the width of the cardboard strip.

Fitting Your Mirrors into Any Tube

It is always better to make your mirror system a little smaller than needed. You can always fill in any gaps between the mirrors and the tube, but it is almost impossible to trim a little off a set of mirrors. If your mirrors are rattling around in the tube, wrap them in craft foam to stabilize them.

Craft foam can keep your mirrors secure inside a large tube.

Angle and Reflection Guide

This guide will help you know the kind of reflections to expect from different mirror configurations.

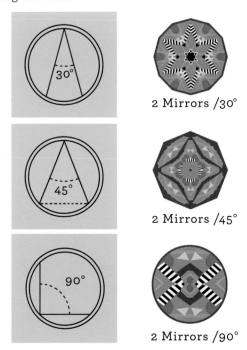

2 Mirrors /30°

2 Mirrors /45°

2 Mirrors /90°

RESOURCES

Fashioning your own versions of end caps, eyeguards, eyepieces, and even object chambers can be easy once you understand the basic structure of a kaleidoscope and how it works. You just have to know what materials to look out for—and keep a close eye on that recycling bin! Here I'll break down for you what kinds of everyday materials you can recycle to make a lean, mean, and—most important—green kaleidoscope.

Kaleidoscope Body

Always be on the lookout for tubes or cylinders that can be turned into a kaleidoscope body. They are everywhere! In the aisles of the supermarket, there are all kinds of products—from lemonade to candy—that are packed in cylinders. How cool is it that you can turn some unwanted materials into your own beautiful kaleidoscope? Here are some ideas to get you started:

- Mailing tubes
- The inner core from a roll of wrapping paper
- Potato chip cans
- Fuzzy paint rollers
- Plastic bird feeders
- Cardboard tubes from plastic wrap and aluminum foil
- Snack containers

- Shampoo bottles
- Water bottles
- Long matchboxes
- Toothpaste boxes
- Cracker boxes
- Milk cartons

Goodies

Almost anything small can be turned into a "goody"—so you should keep an eye out all the time for goodies that are small enough to fit inside the object chamber. Be creative: The most exciting objects to look at will be transparent or translucent, so that the light can pass through the objects and make a brighter image in your scope. (Opaque objects will show up as a silhouette.) Dollar, party, and crafts stores have all kinds of trinkets. Pay close attention in the supermarket, the drug store, or look in the junk drawer in your house . . . You never know where the next treasure is hiding.

Objects with definitive shape or texture, such as a few wisps of a cotton ball, can create interesting silhouettes. Words and pictures printed on clear recycled plastic or thin paper will spill secret messages all over the inside of the scope. Here are some zt zother ideas:

- Small plastic bugs
- Tiny gears and springs
- Old watch parts
- Screws
- Hex nuts
- Lace
- Gumball-machine toys
- Key chains
- Rubber bands
- Paper clips
- Safety pins
- Uncooked pasta
- Doll accessories
- Springs from a ballpoint pen
- Mardi Gras beads
- Old costume jewelry

End Caps

Almost any kind of cap from various kinds of packaging will work as an end cap. If you get desperate, you can always use a piece of clear, flat plastic, and tape it where you

FROM TRASH TO TREASURE

Besides the usual stuff that you might accumulate for your object chambers—like tiny plastic charms, barrettes, brightly colored jacks, and tiny novelty erasers—don't forget that sometimes a scope chamber is the perfect place to reuse *broken* objects that would otherwise be on their way to the trash, such as:

- Bingo chips
- Broken bits of colored plastic
- Buttons
- Clear dice that have lost their board games
- Cut-up bits of colored cellophane, tissue paper, drinking straws, plastic tubing, plastic bags, mesh vegetable bags, packaging labels, translucent or clear party cups, goodie bags
- Glass nuggets used in floral arrangements
- Old toys
- Plastic toothpicks
- Teeth of an old comb

need it to go. Otherwise, keep these in mind when you need an end cap:

- Laundry detergent caps
- Clear plastic rug protectors (also known as casters)
- Spray-can lids
- Mint containers
- Coasters or floor protectors for furniture legs

Eyepieces

Your basic eyepiece is usually going to be a lid or a cap with a hole in the center. (Get an adult to cut or drill the hole for you.) But you may also be able to use a foam can holder—often available in the foam aisle in a crafts shop or another novelty store. Because it's made of foam, it will be soft on your face, and it already has a hole in the middle! Stretch it to fit whatever tube you're using as a scope body.

Object Chambers

Have you ever put a quarter in a vending machine and won a shiny ring or tiny stuffed animal? If the prize came in a plastic egg-shaped container, use the container as a chamber (and use the top as an end cap!). Here are some other materials you could use as an object chamber:

- Small round bead boxes from crafts shops

- Plastic drink cups, old yogurt containers, snack packages
- Clear medicine jars, spice jars, baby food jars
- A slice of cardboard tube with a clear plastic bottom taped on

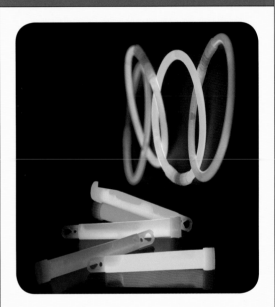

SPARKS IN THE DARK

The glow sticks we get at parties and wear as bracelets and necklaces will make an amazing light show in your scope. (Remember that they are temporary and, after the glow has dimmed, should be discarded.)

For other luminous ideas, check out novelty stores—they sell light-up cups, coasters, pins, necklaces, and other decorations. Or hold up some glow-in-the-dark stickers to a light to "charge" them, then immediately put them in the object chamber. Did you ever get a flashing pin or ring at a party? Make it blink and put it into the chamber.

If you can't find some sort of ready-made chamber, you can always make one from two clear water bottles. Simply cut off the bottom of each water bottle, insert your goodies, and tape the two bottoms together around the seam.

Mirrors

It might seem like recyclable mirror materials would be hard to come by, but you will be surprised at how many reflective surfaces you can find practically right before your eyes. Inspect the plastic from leftover packaging. Look at discarded containers. Save the large clear to-go boxes from a salad bar—they're great to work with. Have you had a birthday? Did the store birthday cake come with a see-through plastic lid? Check that out.

Keep in mind that some of these supplies should be reinforced with pieces of black paper or cardboard to make them rigid. Or, you can easily prepare a whole sheet of mirror by pressing a sheet of black adhesive foam to a piece of plastic that's the same size. Here are some more ideas for alternative mirror materials:

- Clear transparency film
- Laminating film (thicker than transparency film)
- Acetate sheets (many copy shops will bind your documents into booklets with clear acetate covers, which can be purchased separately and are a bit thicker than transparency film)

LOOK FOR GOODIES IN NATURE

Some of the things suggested here might be a bit delicate, but it's worth a try to see the lacey designs that Mother Nature's creations may make in your scope. Because symmetry is part of so many plants, they often look especially interesting when their shapes are multiplied. They won't stay fresh for long in your scope, though, so don't forget to remove them.

- **Flora:** Try out tiny dried flowers, petals, small pinecones, pine needles, tendrils, and seeds. Or search the pantry for dried beans, grains, and seeds.

- **Minerals:** Clear or colored crystals, such as amethyst or rose quartz, that are small enough to fit in the object chamber (usually less than ½" across) can make beautiful designs. Lots of gift shops and museum stores sell semiprecious stones by the piece or the bag.

- **Sea life:** Everyone likes to search for shells on the beach. Tiny seashells, pebbles, and beach glass will make the image inside your scope as organic as the real thing.

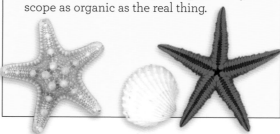

- Clear craft plastic
- Clear plastic shrink film
- Piece of black cardboard laminated or covered with clear packing tape
- Gift cards (Crazy, but true! Slice the reflective cards into three equal strips. You'll be surprised at the pretty decent result.)
- Mirror board and mirror paper, which is basically cardstock with a highly reflective side (it is easy to cut with scissors and available in crafts stores with scrapbooking supplies)

And last, but not least . . . look inside your potato chip bag. In most potato chip bags, you'll see a mirror-ized surface. But I don't have to tell you not to stick your head in the bag to see it. Instead, when the bag is empty, flatten it and trim off the bottom and sides to make two flat pieces. Just as we try to get as much light into our scopes as possible, the opposite applies to foods. The mirrored coating blocks light waves and moisture that can make the chips stale. What a great way to recycle!

Wheels

There are endless possibilities for crafting kaleidoscope wheels. From a simple circular lid to a goofy creation made from a sink drainer, wheels are another kaleidoscope element that are all around us. Of course, you could always cut a circle from cardboard, heavy paper, recycled plastic, colored foam, or any other flat, sturdy material. The only part of the wheel that you will see reflected is the part that passes in front of the perimeter of the mirrors. So a giant wheel might look neat, but you will only see a small portion of it. Here are some suggestions for wheel materials:

- Old CDs, the clear protective CD at the top of a new package (this option will need a large axle), or any part of the packaging from a stack of CDs
- Disposable plastic plates
- Lids from round take-out containers or to-go cups
- Clear or translucent lids from margarine, yogurt, or deli containers
- Plastic canvas for needlepoint, available in circles from crafts shops (weave yarn, ribbon, and beads and attach brightly colored buttons to decorate it appropriately)
- Disposable cardboard coasters
- Small doilies
- Sun catchers painted to look like stained glass
- Plastic stamp templates (used in scrapbooking)

Keep in mind: A kaleidoscope's "wheel" does not necessarily have to be round! It can be any shape, as long as the hole for viewing is covered. A square plastic CD sleeve or even a triangle (as long as it's big enough) will work.

METRIC CONVERSIONS

Use These Formulas for Precise Conversions:
Inches × 2.54 = centimeters
Feet × .304 = meters

INCHES	CENTIMETERS	INCHES	CENTIMETERS
½	1.3	8	20.3
1	2.5	8½	21.6
1½	3.8	9	22.9
2	5.1	9½	24.1
2½	6.4	10	25.4
3	7.6	11	27.9
3½	8.9	12	30.5
4	10.2	13	33.0
4½	11.4	14	35.6
5	12.7	15	39.1
5½	14.0	16	40.6
6	15.2	17	43.2
6½	16.5	18	45.7
7	17.8	19	48.3
7½	19.1	20	50.8

FEET	METERS	FEET	METERS
1	.304	3½	1.064
1½	.456	4	1.216
2	.608	4½	1.368
2½	.760	5	1.520
3	.912		

CONCLUSION

Your journey through this book may have come to an end, but your kaleidoscope journey will go on forever. Keep the wheels of science, light, optics, color, and knowledge spinning round and round, and your life will be *kaleidoscopic*!

ACKNOWLEDGMENTS

I would like to thank my late parents, Arnold and Bertha Bennett, for the love and support that allowed me to travel an unconventional path to my dreams; Dawn Baker, the right arm that keeps my kaleidoscopes spinning, and the sister who can turn any chaos to calm; the many friends and family who have been with me on the kaleido-journey and applauded all along the way; and Cozy Baker, without whom there would not be a kaleidoscope community—she was our guide and inspiration. The Brewster Kaleidoscope Society continues her legacy.

I would also like to acknowledge the late Peter Workman. The company he built and the vision he had for allowing artists and writers to share their stories made writing this book possible. Finally, thank you to Liz Davis, Tae Won Yu, and all the members of the Workman team who helped make this book a reality.

I live in a world of music, light, color, and nature. I could not make kaleidoscopes without any of them.

JOIN THE BREWSTER KALEIDOSCOPE SOCIETY

If you love kaleidoscopes and would like to learn even more about them, you can find the Brewster Kaleidoscope Society on the Web at BrewsterSociety.com. The BKS is an organization made up of kaleidoscope designers and collectors and lovers of kaleidoscopes.